back porch paleo

Homestyle Comfort Food
from Our Table to Yours

Michelle Daniels and Makenna Homer

creators of back porch paleo

PAGE STREET
PUBLISHING CO.

PAGE STREET
PUBLISHING CO.

First published in 2021 by
Page Street Publishing Co.
27 Congress Street, Suite 105
Salem, MA 01970
www.pagestreetpublishing.com

Distributed by Macmillan, sales in Canada by The Canadian Manda Group.

25   24   23   22   21   1   2   3   4   5

ISBN-13: 978-1-64567-402-3
ISBN-10: 1-64567-402-9

Library of Congress Control Number: 2021931972

Cover and book design by Meg Baskis for Page Street Publishing Co.
Photography by Michelle Daniels and Makenna Homer

Printed and bound in the United States

dedication

To DeVona and Patsy for giving us the wings to fly through this amazing journey without you being here to guide us. We miss you both so very much.

contents

Foreword

I met Michelle and Makenna of Back Porch Paleo a couple of years ago through the Whole30 community and was instantly enamored by the passion they poured into everything they did. Michelle is a warm and gracious mother, blogger and influencer who creates delicious food with a mission to help heal her daughter. The sort of mom-hug she exudes and the way she embraces one and all speak deeply to me. As a parent, and as a woman who also infuses food with love, I am drawn in by that kind of magic. And as a Whole30-endorsed cookbook author, I see evidence of that magic throughout their beautiful cookbook.

As I grew to learn Michelle and Makenna's story and learn more about the healing journey of their family, our connection deepened. I treasure our shared territory of taking care of people through food and translating family recipes into more healthful, yet delicious, versions. I find their out-of-the-box comfort food absolutely fantastic, and I love this mother-daughter duo and their mission!

More than anything I would enjoy an opportunity to be on that back porch with Michelle, Makenna and their family. You know that feeling of eating the food from your grandmother's kitchen? Somehow, they have managed to infuse this level of nurturing into their recipes, and it truly is a gift.

Michelle and Makenna have a knack for updating family classics to be more healthful, but not crazy restrictive. Committed Paleo eaters as well as the Paleo-curious will find some exciting variety here, as well as permission to explore. I am thrilled to say that although there's never a moment when I feel I'm eating "health" food, I clearly notice how exceptionally well I feel after eating Michelle and Makenna's creations. They take everyday eating up a notch with dishes that are special and delicious and speak to a time when families gathered around the table sharing stories and laughter.

This book is an amazing guide to a healthful, grain-free, Paleo-ish way of cooking that still exudes the kind of lusciousness that you want to gather around a table and enjoy. There's so much to choose from: breakfast as a lifestyle, family dinners, potluck favorites and desserts, to name a few. And I love the idea of serving festive beverages, which simply make life more fun— and let's face it, who doesn't need a little bit more of that?

Teri Turner,
author of the bestselling cookbook *No Crumbs Left*, founder of
the popular blog NoCrumbsLeft and podcaster

Introduction

Hi there, friends! We're so happy that you found your way to our book and are interested in reading about our journey. We truly appreciate you being here.

We are Michelle and Makenna, a mother-daughter duo, and we are so excited to share our Paleo foodie story and the journey it has taken us on. Ready your taste buds. We have re-created what we think are some pretty fantastic family favorites and the ultimate comfort foods we thought we'd never be able to enjoy again.

Makenna's health took a severe turn after she graduated from high school. She was quickly diagnosed with Crohn's disease and, after multiple failed medication treatment plans, we turned to food as one of the tools we could use to help her heal. We had used this method before due to a pretty serious scare she'd had in fifth grade with psoriasis. Psoriasis is inflammation on the outside, so with her new diagnosis of Crohn's disease—inflammation on the inside—we thought food could once again be the missing link.

For us, this meant eliminating inflammatory trigger foods like refined sugars, gluten, dairy and legumes. This way of eating is commonly known as the Paleo diet. We removed these foods and shifted our focus to incorporating whole and nutrient-dense foods. Slowly but surely, Makenna started to feel improvement in her health and began regaining her energy.

Our diet before this crisis was pretty close to the standard American diet, so drastically changing what we ate meant that we lost quite a few of our favorite family recipes. It became our mission to re-create these nostalgic recipes, in a way that our bodies would enjoy. We found that cassava flour is an excellent substitute for wheat flour, maple sugar provides a wonderful sweetness and vegetables don't have to be boring! Food became exciting again as we found new ways to make these comforting recipes, and it has brought us to where we are today.

Our heavenly angels have been so crucial in this journey. As you work your way through our recipes, you'll notice two names mentioned: DeVona and Patsy. DeVona was Michelle's sweet mother and Makenna's incredible grandma. Patsy was Michelle's kind mother-in-law and Makenna's second unbelievable grandma. DeVona was a pioneer in the health industry with her health radio show of 25 years, and Patsy was the original kitchen diva and a culinary genius. While both of these marvelous women are no longer with us on this earth, their spirits and presence have guided us through this complicated journey. From advocating for ourselves in the health realm to learning the tricks of the trade in recipe development, we would not be where we are today without them. We are endlessly thankful for their guidance and miss them every single day.

Our blog name, Back Porch Paleo, is not an accident. The "back porch" vibe is our family in a nutshell. We are all about gathering whoever's available at the time to chill, enjoy great food and laugh a lot. It's not uncommon to have extended family, neighbors and friends drop by unannounced and enjoy whatever we are currently eating. They know where to find the muffins in the freezer, and they will forage in the fridge for leftovers. We are a very accepting and unconditionally loving bunch, and you will find us on our back porch most summer evenings, enjoying something extraordinary that just came off the grill.

Comfort food is basically our middle name. We sincerely hope that when you make these recipes, you'll be able to feel the love that's gone into the remakes of some of our most beloved family dishes. Many of them do take extra time to make, but we feel that spending time in the kitchen preparing food with loved ones is time well spent. Some of our most cherished memories happen in the kitchen.

Welcome to our kitchen table!

Michelle Daniels

Makenna Homer

Our QR code will take you to our website where you can find several instructional video tutorials. Sometimes it's helpful to watch for visual tips on a few trickier recipes, like Paleo Pie Crust (page 131). Simply scan with the camera on your smartphone!

A Few Thoughts on
Our Paleo Journey

To say we've evolved over the past eight years on our family health journey would be an understatement. Our Paleo journey started when Makenna got sick after high school and we were searching for answers. After many efforts to help her via the medical route, we were stumped and not seeing improvement. When we decided to go Paleo in January 2014, we embraced the diet's guidelines as strictly as we could so she could heal. We looked at all the dos and don'ts of living a Paleo lifestyle and followed them to the letter, since Makenna's health at that time demanded it. We have no regrets about that whatsoever. We needed the guidelines to get her health on the right track.

Now here we are in 2021. Does the way we eat now look similar to how we ate in 2014? Of course, and for good reason. We've learned what works for our bodies and what doesn't. Why abandon the tools that have served us so well? Now, does the way we eat also look *different* than it did in 2014? Absolutely. There is a constant influx of new information, products, friends, podcasts and even medications, and our bodies also evolve and heal. To not incorporate the knowledge and again listen to our bodies would be a mistake.

With that said, our Paleo template may look different from yours at this point, and that's okay. In fact, we think that's awesome and very relevant. Everyone's body is different, period. There is not a one-size-fits-all approach to healing. How could there be? If living this lifestyle has taught us anything, it's that we always need to allow space for the effort and work that anyone puts into thriving.

There are a few things in our book that may look different from the Paleo way of eating that you're used to, based on how our template has evolved. You'll see a couple of recipes with basmati rice, organic powdered sugar and even grass-fed butter.

This book is a snapshot of what our evolved Paleo lifestyle looks like at this moment, and it could change in a few months as we listen to our doctors and our bodies. That's the main point we're hoping to convey here: It's okay to evolve as you learn and as your body heals and adjusts. Using the Paleo guidelines as a template for healing and good health has outstanding merit and benefits. Our health journey is better because of it, and we will continue to live it.

comfy morning eats

We are firm believers that a good day cannot begin without a delicious breakfast. For many years, as kids went to school and parents went to work, the morning would start around the kitchen bar, with the family eating breakfast together. In the fast-paced world we exist in nowadays, we found this was a fantastic way to take a deep breath and muster the energy to tackle the day head-on. Although our family members are all in their own homes now, it's comforting to know that even apart, we're all still sitting down for breakfast to start our days.

The very first recipe in this chapter, Patsy's Pumpkin–Chocolate Chip Muffins (page 16), is a recipe near and dear to our hearts. This was often the go-to breakfast around that kitchen bar. To remake it in a gut-friendly way was one of the first challenges we tackled, and we think we absolutely nailed it—the oozy chocolate, the pumpkin spice and, of course, the beautiful muffin top. You'll find both sweet and savory breakfasts in this chapter because every morning we wake up wanting something a little different. Regardless of your flavor preference, there's definitely breakfast in here for you. We hope you enjoy every single one!

patsy's pumpkin–chocolate chip muffins

If a muffin could talk, this one would say, "I'm the favorite," and it would not be wrong. Not only is it our family favorite but it's also the favorite of many of our neighbors and friends. Our Patsy was famous for her muffins, and this pumpkin–chocolate chip offering was her most requested. It was the very first muffin to be remade Paleo and posted on our blog, followed by over a dozen more. We make this recipe year-round, for good reason. The warm aroma of spices that fills our kitchen while they bake makes it very hard to wait until they're done. Enjoying one after they come out of the oven while the chocolate chips are still warm rivals any other Paleo muffin experience and will have you making these muffins again and again.

yield: 8 to 9 large muffins

1¼ cups (166 g) cassava flour

¾ cup (141 g) maple sugar

1 tbsp (6 g) pumpkin pie spice

1 tsp baking soda

½ tsp fine sea salt

¼ tsp baking powder

1 cup (168 g) dairy-free dark chocolate chips

3 large eggs, at room temperature

1 tsp pure vanilla extract

½ cup (120 ml) melted ghee or grass-fed butter

1 cup (245 g) plain pumpkin puree

Preheat the oven to 385°F (196°C). Line a large muffin tin with parchment baking liners and set it aside.

In a medium bowl, whisk together the cassava flour, maple sugar, pumpkin pie spice, baking soda, salt and baking powder. Add the chocolate chips and stir to combine the ingredients, then set the flour mixture aside.

In a small bowl, whisk together the eggs, vanilla, ghee and pumpkin puree until everything is well combined and the eggs are all incorporated. Add the egg mixture to the flour mixture and stir to combine them with a rubber spatula.

Scoop the batter into the prepared muffin tin; you should get eight to nine muffins, depending on how large you like your muffins. Bake the muffins for 22 to 24 minutes, or until a toothpick inserted into the center of a muffin comes out clean.

Remove the muffins from the oven, let them sit in the tin for 5 minutes and then carefully transfer them to a cooling rack to cool completely.

Enjoy the muffins the same day or store them in the refrigerator for up to 1 week. These muffins freeze well and can thaw to room temperature sitting on the counter. You may also warm them in the microwave: If you are warming room-temperature muffins, microwave them for 20 to 30 seconds. If you are warming frozen muffins, microwave them for 45 to 60 seconds.

saturday morning donuts

Like most families, we are huge fans of the weekend. What better way to celebrate the start of two days off than heading to the local bakery and picking up a dozen of your favorite donuts to share? Glazed, jelly-filled and cruller donuts were all delicious; however, we were particularly fond of the cake donuts with sprinkles. They are incredibly delicious and also adorable. Between the gluten and the sugar, though, donuts slowly disappeared from our Saturday morning routines once we adopted a Paleo diet, which was extremely sad. We developed this recipe to bring donuts back to our weekends. You better believe they're back in the rotation, and we couldn't be happier about it.

yield: 18 mini donuts

donuts

1 cup (133 g) cassava flour
1 tsp baking powder
¼ tsp fine sea salt
2 tbsp (24 g) maple sugar
¼ cup (57 g) ghee
1 large egg, at room temperature
¼ cup (60 ml) pure maple syrup, at room temperature
¾ cup (180 ml) plain unsweetened almond milk, at room temperature
1 tsp pure vanilla extract

glaze

1 cup (120 g) organic powdered sugar or maple powdered sugar
2 tbsp (30 ml) almond milk
Sprinkles (optional)

To make the donuts, whisk together the cassava flour, baking powder and salt in a medium bowl. Set the flour mixture aside.

In another medium bowl, combine the maple sugar and ghee. Using a hand mixer, beat them together until they are well combined. Add the egg, maple syrup, almond milk and vanilla and mix again until all the ingredients are well incorporated.

Add the flour mixture to the maple sugar–ghee mixture, and then mix again until they are thoroughly combined. To more easily fill the donut maker, add the batter to a 1-gallon (3.8-L) bag and snip off one corner.

Prepare the donut maker according to the manufacturer's directions. Bake the donuts for 5 to 7 minutes, until they are golden brown, then transfer them to a cooling rack. We use a Babycakes brand donut maker and get about 18 donuts. Alternatively, you can use a mini donut baking pan and bake the donuts at 375°F (191°C) for 15 to 17 minutes, until they are golden brown. Allow the donuts to cool on a cooling rack.

While the donuts are cooling, mix up the glaze by placing the powdered sugar and milk in a small bowl. Mix them together until they are smooth. When the donuts are cool, dip them into the glaze one at a time, allowing the excess glaze to drip back into the bowl. Place the donuts back on the cooling rack. Decorate the donuts with the sprinkles (if using) before the glaze sets.

Alternatively, you can be creative and mix about ½ cup (69 g) of cooked sausage or bacon into the batter or even ½ cup (84 g) of chopped chocolate or ½ cup (10 g) of freeze-dried fruit before baking. If you choose to use maple powdered sugar for the glaze, it will have a stronger caramel color and maple flavor.

maple-bacon muffins

This particular variety of muffin is a special one. Not only are the flavors incredible—what goes together better than maple and bacon?—but they are full of memories. While Makenna was in high school, her friends would frequently come over and raid the freezer for any muffin they could get their hands on. These Maple-Bacon Muffins were one of the most popular among her friends, and we regularly received requests to make more when they ran out. If we put the perfect breakfast into a muffin, it would be this. Just be careful, because we're pretty sure they'll disappear extremely fast after you make them!

yield: 8 large or 10 standard muffins

muffins

1 cup (240 ml) almond milk

1 tbsp (15 ml) fresh lemon juice

1¾ cups (233 g) cassava flour

½ cup (94 g) maple sugar, plus additional for dusting (optional)

1 tsp baking soda

¼ tsp fine sea salt

3 large eggs, at room temperature

¼ cup (60 ml) melted ghee, slightly cooled

1 tsp pure vanilla extract

¼ cup (60 ml) plain nondairy yogurt

1 cup (225 g) roughly chopped cooked bacon, divided

Preheat the oven to 385°F (196°C) and line a standard muffin tin with parchment baking liners.

To make the muffins, first whisk together the almond milk and lemon juice in a small bowl. Let the mixture sit for 5 minutes. The result is almond milk "buttermilk."

In a medium bowl, whisk together the cassava flour, maple sugar, baking soda and salt. Set the flour mixture aside.

Crack the eggs into another medium bowl. Whisk them until they are frothy and well combined. Add the almond milk "buttermilk", ghee, vanilla and yogurt. Whisk again to fully combine all the ingredients.

Pour the egg-milk mixture into the flour mixture, along with ¾ cup (169 g) of the bacon. Mix the ingredients together with a rubber spatula until everything is combined.

Scoop the batter into the prepared muffin tin. If you want larger muffins with a glorious muffin top, fill eight of the liners. If you want standard-sized muffins, you can fill up to ten or eleven of the liners. If desired, you can sprinkle the top of each with a little bit of additional maple sugar.

Bake the muffins for 18 to 22 minutes, or until the edges are golden brown and the centers are set. Remove the muffins from the oven and let them sit in the tin for 4 minutes, or until they are cool enough to handle, then transfer them to a cooling rack.

(continued)

maple-bacon muffins (cont.)

glaze

¼ cup (60 ml) melted ghee
¼ cup (60 ml) pure maple syrup
¼ cup (51 g) coconut sugar
⅛ tsp fine sea salt

While the muffins bake, make the glaze by combining the ghee, maple syrup, coconut sugar and salt in a small saucepan. Warm this mixture over low heat until the coconut sugar is melted, then add the remaining ¼ cup (56 g) of bacon. Remove the saucepan from the heat and set it aside.

When you are ready to serve the muffins, place a warm muffin on a plate and pour about 1 tablespoon (15 ml) of the warm glaze over the muffin. Dig in!

These muffins are best enjoyed warm from the oven with the glaze. They're perfect for a slow Saturday morning or holiday breakfast. Store any leftover muffins and glaze in the refrigerator and enjoy them within 2 days.

biscuits 'n' gravy

This meal is a blast from the past that says "comfort food" to so many people. Your average recipe for biscuits and gravy is full of gluten and dairy, which simply won't do for our sensitive stomachs. This new Paleo twist is so delicious and also gut-friendly! You can once again enjoy a warm biscuit topped with creamy sausage gravy. You'll have everyone running to the kitchen with the aromas of biscuits baking and savory sausage gravy simmering. This is a quintessential weekend or holiday breakfast meal that is sure to be on repeat.

yield: 6 biscuits

biscuits

1 tsp fresh lemon juice

⅓ cup (80 ml) full-fat coconut milk

1 cup (133 g) plus 2 tbsp (16 g) cassava flour, divided, plus additional as needed

2 tsp (8 g) baking powder

½ tsp salt

¼ cup (57 g) grass-fed butter, cut into ½" (1.3-cm) pieces

1 large egg

1 large egg for wash (optional)

2 tbsp (30 ml) water

To make the biscuits, line a medium baking sheet with parchment paper or a silicone baking mat.

In a small bowl, combine the lemon juice and coconut milk. Stir to combine them and set the bowl aside. This mixture will turn into "buttermilk."

In a medium bowl, use a fork to combine 1 cup (133 g) of the cassava flour, baking powder and salt. Add the butter and cut it into the dry ingredients with a pastry blender or your fingers until the mixture resembles coarse crumbs.

Stir the buttermilk. Whisk in 1 of the eggs to combine it with the buttermilk. Make a well in the center of the flour mixture, then pour the buttermilk-egg mixture into the flour mixture. Stir the two until they are combined and the dough comes together.

Lay a medium piece of parchment paper on a flat work surface and lightly dust it with additional cassava flour. Shape the dough into a square and, with your hands, flatten it until it is approximately 1 inch (2.5 cm) thick. Put the remaining 2 tablespoons (16 g) of cassava flour in a small bowl and dip the edge of a 2-inch (5-cm) biscuit or cookie cutter into the flour to coat it. Press the biscuit cutter straight down into the dough—*do not twist the cutter*. Tap the cutter in your hand to remove the biscuit, and then place it on the prepared baking sheet. Repeat this process with the remaining dough, reshaping the dough and cutting out the biscuits until you use all the dough. You should get six to seven 2-inch (5-cm) biscuits.

(continued)

biscuits 'n' gravy (cont.)

sausage gravy

1 tbsp (15 ml) avocado oil or melted ghee

½ cup (80 g) diced sweet onion

¾ cup (130 g) cooked sausage, crumbled

¾ tsp fine sea salt

¼ tsp garlic powder

2 tbsp (16 g) cassava flour

1¾ cups (420 ml) almond milk

1 tbsp (15 ml) fresh lemon juice

⅛ tsp fish sauce

1 tbsp (3 g) finely chopped fresh chives (optional)

Black pepper, as needed

Place 2 tablespoons (30 ml) of water in a small bowl. Dip your finger into the water and slowly wipe the water over the top of each biscuit until its surface is smooth.

A little water is all you need; more is not better in this case. Take your time during this process. Place the baking sheet in the refrigerator for 15 minutes.

Preheat the oven to 450°F (232°C) while the biscuits chill. Remove the biscuits from the fridge. If using the optional egg wash, add the remaining egg to a small cup; whisk until combined. Then, brush the top of each biscuit with the egg wash. Bake the biscuits for 12 to 15 minutes, until they are golden brown on top.

Remove the biscuits from the oven and let them cool slightly before serving them. Use your fingers or a fork to separate them. They are best the day you make them but can be frozen.

To make the sausage gravy, heat a 10-inch (25-cm) cast-iron skillet over medium heat. Add the avocado oil. Stir in the onion and sauté it over medium heat until it is soft and slightly golden.

Add the sausage, salt and garlic powder, stirring the ingredients to combine them. Sprinkle the cassava flour over the mixture and stir to coat the ingredients.

Pour in the almond milk and whisk the mixture for 5 to 6 minutes, until it has thickened. Stir in the lemon juice, fish sauce, chives (if using) and black pepper. Serve the gravy on each half of the split biscuits.

cinnamon-sugar mini muffins

Cinnamon and sugar are a match made in heaven, and we can never get enough! Combine those flavors with these adorable mini muffins, and you have a cute and scrumptious morning treat. In our house, we believe muffins belong in the breakfast rotation, and these delightfully sweet treats are the perfect complement to some savory bacon and eggs. We've never encountered someone who hasn't been a massive fan of these. Keep them all for yourself, or share them with others if you can bear to let any go!

yield: 18 mini muffins

muffins

1 cup (133 g) cassava flour

1 tsp baking powder

½ tsp fine sea salt

½ tsp ground cinnamon

½ cup (94 g) maple sugar

⅓ cup (64 g) organic vegetable shortening

1 large egg, at room temperature

1 tsp pure vanilla extract

½ cup (120 ml) full-fat coconut milk, at room temperature

cinnamon-sugar coating

¼ cup (60 ml) melted grass-fed butter

½ cup (94 g) maple sugar

2 tsp (6 g) ground cinnamon

To make the muffins, preheat the oven to 350°F (177°C). Spray a mini muffin tin with avocado oil.

In a small bowl, whisk together the cassava flour, baking powder, salt and cinnamon until they are fully combined. Set the flour mixture aside.

In a medium bowl, use a hand mixer to cream together the maple sugar and shortening for about 1 minute, until the mixture is fluffy and well combined. Add the egg and vanilla and mix the ingredients well.

Alternate adding one-third of the flour mixture with one-third of the coconut milk, mixing well after each addition, until everything is well combined. Fill the muffin wells three-fourths full. Bake the muffins for 15 to 17 minutes, or until the edges just begin to turn brown and the centers are set. Remove the muffins from the oven and let them cool completely in the muffin tin.

While the muffins bake, prepare the cinnamon-sugar coating. Place the butter in a small bowl and the maple sugar and cinnamon in another small bowl. Once the muffins are cool, take a muffin and dip the top into the melted butter. Allow any excess butter to drip off. Then press the muffin's top into the cinnamon-sugar coating. Repeat this process with the remaining muffins. If you prefer to dip the entire muffin, you will need to double the coating ingredients.

These are best the day they're made, but they can be frozen as well for up to a month. Store any uneaten muffins at room temperature for up to 2 days.

speckled vanilla bean scones

Like many people, we used to swing by our local Starbucks in the morning to grab a Vanilla Bean Crème Frappuccino® paired with a vanilla bean scone. This breakfast option was fast, convenient and boy, were those scones tasty. To no one's surprise, loading yourself up with that much sugar in the morning does not typically make for the best start to your day. We cut that habit out many years ago, but we sure missed those delectable little scones. These lovely vanilla-speckled delights are a much healthier option, and we're happy to say we didn't sacrifice flavor to achieve this!

yield: 12 scones

1 vanilla bean, seeds scraped out and divided

¾ cup (180 ml) full-fat coconut milk

1 cup (133 g) plus 6 tbsp (48 g) cassava flour, plus additional as needed

⅓ cup (63 g) maple sugar

2½ tsp (10 g) baking powder

¼ tsp fine sea salt

½ cup (114 g) grass-fed butter, chilled and cut into ½" (1.3-cm) pieces

1 large egg

2½ cups (330 g) organic powdered sugar or maple powdered sugar

Preheat the oven to 350°F (177°C). Line a medium baking sheet with parchment paper or a silicone baking mat.

Place the vanilla bean seeds in a small bowl, reserving a pinch for making the glaze. Add the coconut milk and whisk to combine it with the vanilla bean seeds. Set this mixture aside.

In a medium bowl, add the cassava flour along with the maple sugar, baking powder and salt. Add the butter and cut it into the dry ingredients with a pastry blender or use your fingers until you have a nice crumbly texture and the butter is combined with the dry ingredients.

Reserve 2 tablespoons (30 ml) of the vanilla milk in a small cup for brushing the scones before baking them. Next, transfer ¼ cup (60 ml) of the vanilla milk to a small bowl for the glaze.

Add the egg to the remaining vanilla milk and whisk them together until they are combined.

Make a well in the middle of the flour mixture and add the egg–vanilla milk mixture. Mix them together using a small wooden spoon until the dough comes together and forms a nice ball, working the dough with your hands as needed.

(continued)

speckled vanilla bean scones (cont.)

Lay a medium piece of parchment paper on a flat work surface and dust it with a bit of additional cassava flour. Place the dough in the middle of the parchment paper and shape the dough into a 6 x 5–inch (15 x 13–cm) rectangle with your hands, pressing it until it is about ¾ inch (2 cm) thick. Using a sharp knife, cut the dough into six rectangles measuring approximately 2 x 2½ inches (5 x 6 cm). Cut these rectangles in half diagonally, giving you twelve scones.

Carefully place each scone on the prepared baking sheet, leaving at least 2 inches (5 cm) between each scone. Using a pastry brush, carefully brush each top with the reserved 2 tablespoons (30 ml) of vanilla milk. Bake the scones for 15 to 17 minutes, or until the edges just begin to turn brown. Remove them from the oven and let them cool completely on the baking sheet.

While the scones are baking, prepare the glaze. Whisk together the reserved ¼ cup (60 ml) of vanilla milk with the remaining pinch of vanilla bean seeds and the powdered sugar. Once the scones are completely cool, carefully dip an upside-down scone into the glaze, letting the excess glaze drip off. Place the scone on a cooling rack to allow the glaze to continue to drip and become firm. Repeat this step with all the scones. Enjoy them once the glaze has firmed up. Store any leftovers at room temperature for up to 2 days.

quick 'n' easy sausage breakfast tacos

Tacos are one of our love languages, and we believe there's no time of day that a taco won't improve. Enter breakfast tacos. These are surprisingly quick and easy to make and hit the spot when you can't find any taco trucks near you in the morning. We think they're the perfect option to whip up for yourself before heading out for the day. Not to mention that the cassava flour tortillas are the best gluten-free tortillas we've ever eaten—you won't miss wheat tortillas. We hope these fuel your mornings just as well as they've fueled ours!

yield: 2 tacos

tortillas

1 cup (133 g) cassava flour
½ tsp fine sea salt
3 tbsp (36 g) organic vegetable shortening
½ cup (120 ml) plus 2 tbsp (30 ml) warm water

To make the tortillas, combine the cassava flour, salt and shortening in a medium bowl. Work all the ingredients together with your fingertips until you have a crumbly mixture.

Add the water and stir the dough mixture with a wooden spoon until it comes together in a ball.

Divide the dough into eight balls and you will have the perfect tortillas for soft tacos; or divide the dough into twelve balls for smaller street tacos. You will need only 2 tortillas for this recipe, but now you have plenty of extra tortillas for all of your other taco endeavors.

Take 1 dough ball and knead it between your hands, then place it between two pieces of 8 x 8–inch (20 x 20–cm) parchment paper. Flatten the dough ball with a tortilla press, roll it out with a rolling pin or flatten it with a small baking sheet. In a dry medium cast-iron skillet over medium-high heat, cook the tortilla for 1 to 3 minutes, until bubbles start to form. Flip it over and do the same for the other side. Remove the tortilla from the skillet and place it on a paper towel. Repeat this step with the remaining dough balls. You can stack the hot tortillas on top of each other or allow them to cool before stacking them.

The tortillas will be stiff after they come off the heat, but they will soften up as they cool. Store any unused tortillas in an airtight bag in the refrigerator for up to 5 days.

(continued)

quick 'n' easy sausage breakfast tacos (cont.)

filling

1 tsp avocado oil or melted ghee
½ cup (69 g) crumbled cooked sausage
2 large eggs
½ tsp ground cumin
½ tsp chipotle chili powder
⅛ tsp fine sea salt

toppings

Garlic-Dill Pickled Onions (page 137)
Avocado, sliced ¼" (6 mm) thick
Chipotle-Tomatillo Salsa (page 142)
2 tsp (1 g) roughly chopped fresh cilantro (optional)

To make the filling, heat a medium cast-iron skillet over medium heat and add the avocado oil. Add the sausage and cook it for 3 to 4 minutes, stirring it occasionally, until it is warmed through and slightly crispy. While the sausage is browning, crack the eggs into a small bowl. Add the cumin, chipotle chili powder and salt, then whisk the ingredients together.

Once the sausage has warmed and browned, add the eggs over the sausage and let them cook until they reach your desired doneness. Try not to agitate the eggs too much, as they're more likely to stick to the skillet that way.

Once the eggs are done to your liking, divide the filling between two of the tortillas. We suggest topping the tacos with our Garlic-Dill Pickled Onions, avocado, our Chipotle-Tomatillo Salsa and cilantro (if using). These tacos are very versatile, so feel free to add leftover potatoes, cheese if you tolerate it or anything else that sounds good. It's pretty hard to mess up a breakfast taco, and we think these are sure to hit the spot.

green chili frittata

Green chili has a permanent seat at every family gathering on Michelle's side of the family. It's always delicious and an effective way to feed a crowd. Our question was, *Why limit that delightful flavor just to dinner?* Thus, the green chili frittata was born. This dish brings all the best aspects of green chili and combines them with the eggy goodness that a big breakfast demands. It's spicy, creamy and very filling. There's enough to feed the family here, so we hope you'll gather around the table and enjoy it together, just as we have time and time again.

yield: 6 servings

12 large eggs, at room temperature

¼ cup (60 ml) dairy-free sour cream

¼ cup (49 g) ghee

1 tsp fine sea salt

2 (4-oz [112-g]) cans diced green chilies

1 tsp ground cumin

½ tsp onion powder

½ tsp garlic powder

¼ tsp chipotle chili powder

1 tbsp (1 g) finely chopped fresh cilantro, divided

1 tbsp (15 ml) avocado oil

2 medium russet potatoes, peeled and cut into ½" (1.3-cm) cubes

½ medium onion, diced

½ cup (75 g) diced red bell pepper

½ cup (100 g) diced green onions

toppings

Chipotle-Tomatillo Salsa (page 142)
Thinly sliced avocado
Thinly sliced green onions
Thinly sliced radishes
Thinly sliced olives

Preheat the oven to 400°F (204°C).

In a large bowl, whisk together the eggs, sour cream, ghee, salt, green chilies, cumin, onion powder, garlic powder, chipotle chili powder and two-thirds of the cilantro. Whisk the ingredients well to ensure all the eggs are fully combined. Set the egg mixture aside.

Heat a 10-inch (25-cm) cast-iron skillet (or another nonstick, oven-safe skillet) over medium heat. Add the avocado oil. Add the potatoes and toss them to coat them in the oil. Sauté the potatoes for 7 to 10 minutes, stirring them occasionally, until most of them have a nice golden color. Add the onion, bell pepper and diced green onions, stirring to mix everything well. Sauté the mixture for 5 to 6 minutes, until the onions and the bell peppers are soft. Remove the skillet from the heat.

Whisk the egg mixture one last time and pour it over the ingredients in the hot skillet, stirring everything together slightly. Place the skillet in the oven and bake the frittata for 15 to 17 minutes, or until it's firm and the center is no longer jiggly.

Remove the frittata from the oven and let it cool slightly, then garnish it with the remaining one-third of the cilantro, Chipotle-Tomatillo Salsa, avocado, sliced green onions, radishes and olives.

breakfast, brunch or brinner waffles

We call these breakfast waffles—but frankly, what meal isn't better when waffles are served? Brunch or "brinner" is always a win. There is just something about a warm waffle right out of the iron, slathered with ghee and a drizzle of warm syrup. We call that "warm, fuzzy food" around here, since so many food memories from our childhoods swirl around our taste buds with the first bite. A round waffle iron has become our favorite shape, since it has built-in pockets that hold whatever you like to spread on top.

Have you tried waffles with pili nuts before? These delicious buttery nuts hail from the Philippines and burst onto the Paleo scene a few years ago. They lend amazing flavor and texture to this batter, which is made super smooth with a blender, while the cassava flour makes these waffles so perfectly Paleo, we're practically giddy about it!

yield: 4 to 5 waffles

1¼ cups (300 ml) coconut milk

4 tsp (20 ml) fresh lemon juice or apple cider vinegar

1 large egg, at room temperature

½ cup (60 g) pili nuts or raw macadamia nuts

¼ cup (60 ml) pure maple syrup, plus additional for serving

¼ cup (60 ml) melted ghee, grass-fed butter or MCT oil

1 tsp pure vanilla extract

1½ tsp (6 g) baking powder

1½ tsp (9 g) fine sea salt

1 cup (133 g) cassava flour

In a small measuring cup, combine the coconut milk and lemon juice and whisk them together. Let the mixture rest for 5 minutes. The result is a coconut milk "buttermilk."

Place the buttermilk, egg, pili nuts, maple syrup, ghee, vanilla, baking powder, salt and cassava flour in a high-powered blender. Blend until the ingredients are well combined and the nuts are smooth.

Preheat a waffle iron. Pour ½ to ¾ cup (120 to 180 ml) of the batter into the waffle iron. Cook the waffle for 4 to 5 minutes—or for the length of time recommended by the waffle iron's manufacturer—until it is golden brown and no longer steaming. Repeat this process with the remaining batter.

Serve the waffles with the toppings of your choice and lots of warm maple syrup.

breakfast enchilada bake

If you love enchiladas and you also happen to love breakfast, then do we have a recipe for you. These breakfast enchiladas are the saucy, spicy and very filling meal of your dreams. This dish will certainly feed a crowd, and for our family, this really hits all of our favorite flavor profiles. This bake is another example of a meal we eat for breakfast, lunch or dinner because it's versatile and delicious no matter the time of day. You can mix and match what toppings you have, add some leftover meat for extra protein or add some cheese if you tolerate it. It's a customizable dish that will end up delicious no matter what.

yield: 6 servings

1 tbsp (15 ml) avocado oil

½ cup (80 g) diced sweet onion

2 cloves garlic, finely chopped

1 (28-oz [784-g]) can organic diced fire-roasted tomatoes, undrained

1 (8-oz [240-ml]) can organic tomato sauce

2 tsp (12 g) fine sea salt, plus additional as needed

2 tsp (4 g) ground cumin

1 tsp dried oregano, rubbed

¼ tsp chipotle chili powder

¼ tsp black pepper, plus additional as needed

1 (7-oz [196-g]) can Herdez® Salsa Casera or salsa of choice

2 cups (480 ml) unsalted chicken bone broth

14 oz (392 g) canned diced green chilies

Juice of 3 medium limes

¼ cup (60 ml) nondairy milk of choice

2 tbsp (16 g) cassava flour

Avocado oil spray, as needed

Warm a 3-quart (2.9-L) saucepan over medium heat. Add the avocado oil, swirling the saucepan to coat the bottom with the oil. Add the onion and cook it for 8 to 10 minutes, stirring it occasionally, until it is soft and the edges are just browned and caramelized. Add the garlic and cook the mixture for 1 to 2 minutes, until the garlic is fragrant, making sure not to burn it.

Add the diced tomatoes with their liquid, tomato sauce, salt, cumin, oregano, chipotle chili powder, black pepper, salsa, bone broth, green chilies and lime juice. Carefully stir the ingredients together until they are well combined. Let the mixture simmer for about 15 minutes so the flavors can mingle. If you like a smoother sauce, at this point, you can use an immersion blender or a food processor to puree the mixture until it is smooth.

To thicken the sauce, make a slurry by stirring together the nondairy milk and cassava flour in a small bowl. While whisking the sauce, slowly pour in the slurry; the mixture should thicken up as you whisk. Stir the sauce to ensure everything is evenly combined, then remove the saucepan from the heat and set it aside.

Preheat the oven to 400°F (204°C). Spray a 12-inch (30-cm) oven-safe skillet with the avocado oil spray. Pour 1 to 1½ cups (240 to 360 ml) of the sauce in the bottom of the skillet and swirl it around to fully coat it with the sauce.

3 (4½-oz [126-g]) bags sea salt plantain chips, plus additional for serving

1 small bunch fresh cilantro, roughly chopped (optional)

2 to 3 green onions, roughly chopped (optional)

Thinly sliced olives (optional)

3 to 4 large eggs

Chipotle chili powder, as needed (optional)

Guacamole, for serving

Chipotle-Tomatillo Salsa (page 142), for serving

Empty 1 bag of the plantain chips into the skillet and distribute them evenly. Pour about 2 cups (480 ml) of the sauce over the plantain chips. Using two forks, move the chips around to coat them well. Repeat this process with the other 2 bags of plantain chips. If you have a little sauce left over, you can add a little more on top. Garnish the chips with the cilantro (if using), green onions (if using) and olives (if using).

Cover the skillet with foil and bake for 20 minutes. Remove the skillet from the oven and remove the foil. Carefully crack the eggs onto the top of the dish, spacing them evenly. Season the eggs with additional salt, black pepper and the chipotle chili powder (if using). Bake the eggs, uncovered, for 8 to 10 minutes, until the egg whites are set but the yolks are still runny and the sauce is bubbly around the edges.

Remove the skillet from the oven and let the enchilada bake cool slightly before serving; it will be very hot and it will slice better if you give it some time to set. Serve it by cutting a slice or simply spooning it out onto individual plates with additional plantain chips, guacamole and Chipotle-Tomatillo Salsa.

Store any leftovers in the fridge for about 1 week.

*See photo on page 14.

what time is dinner?

The members of our family are somewhat obsessed with each other. We're together as often as possible, and it's always better if there's food involved. Naturally, that means we are huge fans of family dinners after busy workdays. Nearly every day of the week was family dinner in our household, and occasionally neighbors, friends and cousins would find their way to our dining table to join the fun. They were smart and knew where to find a good meal when they were out and about. In our eyes, the more, the merrier! We love the unity that a fabulous dinner can bring to a group of people.

All those people who would find their way into our home for dinner? They were drawn in by some of our family's favorite meals, which were on a frequent rotation on our weekly menus. However, when our health journey began, we had to overhaul those well-loved recipes to be more gut-friendly and nutrient-dense. In this chapter, you'll find healthy homemade soups that we used to buy in cans, a delightfully herby Sunday pot roast (page 52), some bacon mac 'n' cheese (page 42) and even a wonderful sloppy joe recipe (page 58)—all old favorites made even tastier with better-for-you ingredients.

Many of the Paleo comfort food recipes in this book have been years in the making, because unless it's the same or better than the original, it's just not worth eating in our eyes. We are thrilled to have these comforting family staples back in our homes and think they'll become a staple in yours as well.

bacon-infused mac 'n' cheese

As a child of the '90s, Makenna consumed many boxes of store-bought mac 'n' cheese. It's a pantry staple for many people, because it's such a quick and easy meal. Homemade Paleo-friendly mac 'n' cheese might sound daunting, but we've worked hard to make this dairy- and gluten-free meal cheesy in taste and simple to make. Not to mention that the addition of bacon really takes this dish to flavor-town. Mac 'n' cheese is back on our dinner rotations, and we could not be more excited about it!

yield: 4 servings

1 cup (146 g) raw unsalted cashews

1 cup (240 ml) water

2 cloves garlic, roughly chopped

2 tbsp (22 g) nutritional yeast

1½ tbsp (23 ml) fresh lemon juice

1½ tsp (8 ml) fish sauce

1 tbsp (15 ml) reserved bacon fat

1 tsp salt

4 oz (112 g) cassava-flour macaroni

3 to 4 strips cooked bacon, roughly chopped, plus additional for garnishing

1 tbsp (3 g) finely chopped fresh chives, plus additional for garnishing (optional)

Black pepper, as needed

In a high-powered blender, combine the cashews, water, garlic, nutritional yeast, lemon juice, fish sauce, bacon fat and salt. Blend the ingredients until all of the cashews are pureed and the mixture is smooth and well combined. Pour the mixture into a small saucepan, and then set the saucepan aside.

Follow the package instructions for preparing the macaroni. When the pasta is nearly finished cooking, warm the "cheese" sauce over low heat for about 5 minutes, stirring it occasionally, until it is warmed through.

Drain the macaroni, then return it to the pan it was cooked in. Pour the warmed sauce over the top. Add the bacon, chives (if using) and black pepper to taste. Stir to combine them with the sauce and pasta. Serve the mac 'n' cheese garnished with the additional bacon and chives (if using) on top.

chicken pesto pita pizza

Pizza! For years after changing the way we ate, we tried so many Paleo-friendly pizza dough variations in search of a recipe that we thought was amazing. We missed pizza so much. This crust recipe finally convinced us that we'd landed on something special. A hybrid between a flatbread and a tortilla, it serves as an excellent vessel for a variety of toppings. You can also grill it, like we do in our recipe for Grilled Hawaiian Vibes Pizza (page 47). For this pesto version, the crusts are cooked either in a cast-iron skillet or on an indoor grill pan, and then toppings are added before warming the pizzas in the oven. Even better, make a few crusts ahead of time for meal prepping, store them in the refrigerator and your weeknight dinner just got that much easier.

yield: 2 (7-inch [18-cm]) individual pizzas

pesto chicken

6 to 7 chicken tenderloins

½ tsp fine sea salt

3 tbsp (45 ml) Toasted Pine Nut Arugula Pesto (page 138), divided

pizza crusts

½ cup (120 ml) plus 2 tbsp (30 ml) plain unsweetened almond milk

2 tbsp (24 g) ghee

¾ cup (100 g) cassava flour, plus additional as needed

½ tsp fine sea salt

¼ tsp garlic powder

Preheat the oven to 400°F (204°C). Line a 13 x 18–inch (33 x 45–cm) baking sheet with parchment paper.

To make the pesto chicken, pat the chicken tenderloins dry with paper towels and place them in a small bowl. Sprinkle the chicken with the salt and add 1 tablespoon (15 ml) of the Toasted Pine Nut Arugula Pesto. Toss the chicken tenderloins to coat them. Allow them to come to room temperature. Cook the chicken tenderloins over medium heat on an indoor grill pan or in a cast-iron skillet until they are no longer pink inside and their internal temperature reaches 165°F (74°C). Place them in a medium bowl and toss them with 2 tablespoons (30 ml) of the Toasted Pine Nut Arugula Pesto to coat them. Set the chicken aside.

To make the pizza crusts, pour the almond milk into a small saucepan and add the ghee. Warm the mixture over low heat until the ghee is just melted, which should take 2 to 3 minutes, but keep an eye on the mixture to make sure it doesn't boil. Remove the saucepan from the heat.

In a small bowl, whisk together the cassava flour, salt and garlic powder. Then pour in the warm almond milk–ghee mixture and stir to combine the ingredients and form a dough. Once the dough is cool enough, pick it up and knead it with your hands until it is a smooth ball.

(continued)

chicken pesto pita pizza (cont.)

pizza crusts (cont.)

Avocado oil spray, as needed

2 tbsp (30 ml) Toasted Pine Nut Arugula Pesto (page 138)

optional toppings

Arugula, as needed

Quartered cherry tomatoes, as needed

Toasted pine nuts, as needed

Crispy pancetta, as needed

Balsamic reduction (page 162), as needed

Lightly dust a medium piece of parchment paper with additional cassava flour. Divide the dough in half—or, if you like a really thin crust, divide the dough into thirds—and place one-half of the dough on the prepared parchment paper, then lay another medium piece of parchment paper on top of the dough. Roll the dough into a circle that is approximately 7 inches (18 cm) in diameter and about ¼ inch (6 mm) thick. Repeat this process with the remaining dough.

Spray the dough with a bit of the avocado oil. Preheat an indoor grill pan or large, dry cast-iron skillet over medium heat. Add one circle of dough, oil side down, to the grill pan and cook the first side for 4 to 6 minutes, until it has some golden-brown spots. Flip the crust over and cook the other side for 3 to 5 minutes. Remove the crust from the pan and set it aside. Repeat this process with the remaining circle of dough.

To assemble the pizzas, spread 1 tablespoon (15 ml) of the Toasted Pine Nut Arugula Pesto on each crust. Shred the pesto chicken and divide it between the crusts, laying the chicken on top of the pesto. Place the crusts on the prepared baking sheet and bake the pizzas for 7 to 9 minutes, or until they are warmed through.

Now, you can add the optional toppings of your choice. We prefer a bit of spicy arugula, cherry tomatoes, toasted pine nuts, pancetta and a drizzle of the balsamic reduction. The possibilities are endless, so add your favorite toppings and serve the pizzas immediately!

grilled hawaiian vibes pizza

Grilling pizza is an all-time favorite summer activity for us. Everyone gets to make their own, so meal prep is shared, and it's so fun to sit on the back porch and visit while the pizzas grill. This is just one variation of what a grilled pizza can be, as the possibilities are endless! Use your favorite red sauce and make a traditional pepperoni pizza. Or add some mashed avocado as the base and top it with cooked taco meat to make a tasty taco pizza with all the fixings—please pass the salsa! No matter the pizza, just be sure all your toppings are precooked, as these beauties grill up in a flash.

yield: 1 (9-inch [23-cm]) pizza or 2 (6-inch [15-cm]) individual pizzas

½ cup (120 ml) marinara or pizza sauce of choice

2 oz (56 g) diced ham or Canadian bacon

½ cup (105 g) roughly chopped fresh or drained canned pineapple

¼ small red onion, thinly sliced

2 tbsp (22 g) thinly sliced black olives

2 tbsp (14 g) sliced almonds

2 tbsp (12 g) thinly sliced green onions (optional)

1 tbsp (1 g) roughly chopped fresh cilantro (optional)

1 to 2 dashes furikake (optional)

1 recipe uncooked pizza crusts (page 45)

Avocado oil, as needed

Pineapple Ranch Dressing (page 57), as needed

Prepare two 13 x 18–inch (33 x 45–cm) baking sheets: Line the first baking sheet with parchment paper. On the second baking sheet, arrange small bowls for holding the marinara sauce, ham, pineapple, red onion, olives, almonds, green onions (if using), cilantro (if using) and furikake (if using). Place the toppings in the bowls. Set both baking sheets aside.

Make the pizza crusts as directed on page 45, but do not cook the dough. Instead, you'll grill the crust. Simply roll out the dough and place it on the parchment paper–lined baking sheet, so it is easy to carry to the grill. Transport both of the baking sheets to your grilling area.

Time to grill the pizza! It's best to have a "pizza station" near the grill with your baking sheets and avocado oil. You will need a long-handled spatula to move the pizza on the grill. Prepare your grill according to the manufacturer's directions, and then preheat the grill to about 400°F (204°C).

Brush one side of the pizza crust with a little of the avocado oil. Lay the oiled side down on the hot grate of the grill. Brush the exposed side of the crust with more avocado oil and close the grill, allowing the heat to swirl around the crust. Cook this side of the crust for 3 to 4 minutes, until it has some grill marks. Flip the crust over with the long-handled spatula and scoot the crust toward yourself, as close to you as possible.

(continued)

grilled hawaiian vibes pizza (cont.)

Working quickly, spread the marinara sauce on the crust. Add the ham, pineapple, red onion and olives. Move the pizza to a cooler spot on your grill with a spatula or reduce the flame if you are using a gas grill. Close the grill's lid again. If the crust is getting too dark on the bottom before the toppings are warmed through, consider turning the grill off, closing the lid and allowing the ambient heat to finish warming the toppings.

The pizza is done when the crust has those nice grill marks on the bottom and the toppings are warmed through. Transfer the pizza to the baking sheet and garnish the pizza with the sliced almonds, green onions (if using) and furikake (if using). Serve the pizza with our Pineapple Ranch Dressing as a sauce for drizzling or dipping.

chipotle-lime steak kebabs

The addition of mango chunks to these kebabs is such a lovely treat, and if you've never had grilled mango before, prepare to be impressed. Be sure to use ripe mangoes, as the cubes will slide onto the skewers more easily and will grill up perfectly. Concerned about the spiciness of the chipotle in this recipe? Don't worry, we've tamed the heat with a very generous amount of lime juice and other seasonings. The chipotle powder simply adds a nice smoky flavor. Remember, with kebabs, it's best to cut all the ingredients to the same size, so that all the pieces have contact with the grill and cook evenly.

yield: **6 to 8 skewers**

1 cup (240 ml) fresh lime juice

1 cup (240 ml) avocado oil

1 tsp ground cumin

1 tsp chili powder

½ tsp garlic powder

½ tsp onion powder

¼ tsp chipotle chili powder

1 tbsp (1 g) finely chopped fresh cilantro, plus additional for topping (optional)

1½ lb (681 g) sirloin steak, cut into 1½" (4-cm) cubes

1 large Ataulfo mango, cut into 1½" (4-cm) cubes

1 medium red onion, cut into 1½" (4-cm) wedges

Kosher salt, for serving (optional)

Lime wedges, for serving (optional)

Mango Steak Sauce (page 149), for serving

Make the marinade by combining the lime juice, avocado oil, cumin, chili powder, garlic powder, onion powder, chipotle chili powder and cilantro (if using) in a large Mason jar or another lidded vessel. Secure the jar's lid and shake well to thoroughly combine the ingredients.

Add the steak cubes to a 6-cup (1.4-L) glass dish or a large ziplock bag. Reserve about ½ cup (120 ml) of the marinade for serving, then pour the rest over the steak. Place the steak in the refrigerator to marinate for a minimum of 6 hours, or up to overnight for optimal flavor.

When you are ready to grill the kebabs, remove the steak from the fridge and allow it to come to room temperature. Meanwhile, if you are using wooden skewers, soak them in water for 15 minutes.

Make the kebabs by threading the steak, mango and red onion wedges onto skewers. Grill the kebabs over high heat on a hot grill pan or outdoor grill until the steak reaches your desired doneness—we cook the kebabs for 4 to 5 minutes per side for medium-rare steak.

Remove the kebabs from the grill pan or grill. Place them on a serving platter. While they are still warm, pour the reserved marinade over them and sprinkle them with the additional cilantro (if using) and kosher salt (if using). Serve the kebabs with the lime wedges (if using) and our Mango Steak Sauce.

herbed sunday pot roast

Every household needs a solid pot roast recipe, and we think you'll understand why this has been our go-to for generations. Countless Sunday dinners in our home have featured this delicious recipe. The aroma of roast beef cooking all day in the slow cooker conjures up all the fond memories of that one day a week when everyone actually sat down together for a slow-paced meal, hoping there would be enough for leftovers the next day. There are a few special tricks that take this pot roast over the top in flavor. The dried mushrooms are full of umami and provide a spectacular depth of flavor that your typical roast just doesn't have. You'll also notice that the onion and garlic are unpeeled. The skins of both lend to the depth of flavor through the cooking process and are strained out after the roast is cooked. This roast is so tender and flavorful, you'll probably end up eating it more often than just at your typical Sunday dinner.

yield: 1 (2- to 2½-lb [908-g to 1.1-kg]) pot roast

roast

1 (2- to 2½-lb [908-g to 1.1-kg])
grass-fed beef chuck roast

4 tsp (24 g) fine sea salt, divided

2 tsp (4 g) onion powder

1 to 2 tbsp (15 to 30 ml) avocado oil

6 baby red potatoes

2 large carrots, peeled and cut into thirds

2 large ribs celery, trimmed and cut into thirds

½ medium onion, unpeeled and cut into wedges

2 to 3 cloves garlic, unpeeled and lightly crushed

1 tsp dried rosemary

¼ cup (7 g) dried porcini mushrooms

3 tbsp (45 ml) apple cider vinegar

4 cups (960 ml) unsalted chicken bone broth, divided

To prepare the roast, place the beef on a plate lined with paper towels. Let the roast come to room temperature and pat the entire roast dry with more paper towels. Season all the sides of the roast with 2 teaspoons (12 g) of the salt and the onion powder.

Warm a 12-inch (30-cm) cast-iron skillet over medium heat. Add the avocado oil and heat it until it's shimmering. Carefully lay the roast in the pan, laying it down facing away from you to avoid a hot oil splatter. Sear the roast on all sides for 3 to 4 minutes per side, or until the meat's surface has a golden-brown sear.

While the roast sears, place the potatoes, carrots, celery, onion, garlic, rosemary, mushrooms and apple cider vinegar in an 8-quart (7.7-L) slow cooker.

When the roast is completely seared, remove it from the skillet and transfer it to the slow cooker. Deglaze the skillet with 1 cup (240 ml) of the bone broth, scraping the bottom of the skillet with a wooden spoon to loosen the cooked-on bits and incorporate them into the broth while being careful to keep your hands away from the steam as it will be quite hot. Pour the bone broth over the roast and veggies. Pour the remaining 3 cups (720 ml) of bone broth over the roast and veggies, nestling the roast into the liquid. If needed, move a few of the veggies around—it's okay if they are along the sides of the roast, as you want the roast to be almost completely submerged. Place the lid on the slow cooker and set it to cook on high for 6 hours.

(continued)

herbed sunday pot roast (cont.)

gravy

Fine sea salt, as needed

Black pepper, as needed

1 sprig fresh rosemary, finely chopped (optional)

2½ tbsp (20 g) cassava flour

6 tbsp (90 ml) water

Splash of balsamic vinegar (optional)

After 6 hours, check the roast for tenderness. It should begin to fall apart with a fork. If needed, place the lid on the slow cooker again and continue to cook the roast for up to 2 more hours. The cooking time will vary a bit, depending on the marbling and thickness of the roast.

Once the roast is done, transfer it to a serving platter along with the potatoes, carrots and celery. Strain the broth into a 3-quart (2.9-L) saucepan, setting the onion wedges on the serving platter if desired and discarding the onion skins and the other solids. You should have approximately 3 to 3½ cups (720 to 840 ml) of broth in the saucepan after straining.

To make the gravy, taste the mixture you strained into the saucepan. Depending on the broth you used, you may need to add more salt, so adjust the salt level accordingly. Add the black pepper and fresh rosemary (if using), then stir the ingredients to combine them and taste the mixture again. Warm this mixture over medium-low heat. While the broth mixture warms, combine the cassava flour and water in a small bowl to make a smooth slurry. While whisking the warm broth, pour in the slurry—the mixture should begin to thicken as you whisk. Reduce the heat to low and add the balsamic vinegar (if using). Stir to combine the vinegar with the gravy.

Serve the pot roast and the veggies with the gravy on the side. You can serve the mashed potatoes from our Cottage Pie (page 65) with this roast.

Instant Pot Instructions: Prepare the roast and the veggies as directed in the recipe and add the ingredients to the inner pot of your Instant Pot®. Cook the roast and veggies at high pressure for 90 to 120 minutes. Allow the pressure to release naturally. Follow the same instructions for preparing the gravy and serving the dish.

p.o.g. chicken on greens

What is this acronym, P.O.G.? If you've not been to Hawaii, it's understandable that you wouldn't know. It stands for the phrase "passion, orange and guava juice." P.O.G. is deliciously refreshing and served everywhere in Hawaii. We have a deep love for island life, and Maui is our favorite place to escape the frigid Utah winters. This salad is an homage to our trips to Hawaii, filled with the flavors that remind us of relaxation, walks on the beach, the warm sun on our cheeks and sipping P.O.G. juice at every opportunity. We marinate the chicken in a delightful blend of these juices along with a few other simple flavors. It's paired with our Pineapple Ranch Dressing, which has a similar flavor profile. We hope you will make this island-inspired meal, enjoy the fragrant flavors and feel that same island vibe.

yield: 4 servings

chicken

2 (8-oz [224-g]) boneless, skinless chicken breasts or 6 (4-oz [112-g]) boneless, skinless chicken thighs

2 cups (480 ml) prepared P.O.G. juice (see sidebar)

¼ cup (60 ml) coconut aminos

¼ cup (60 ml) avocado oil

2 tbsp (26 g) coconut sugar

1½ tsp (9 g) fine sea salt

1 tsp garlic powder

¼ tsp ground ginger

1 green onion, thinly sliced

To prepare the chicken, add it to a 1-gallon (3.8-L) ziplock bag or a large glass container with a lid. In a medium bowl, whisk together the P.O.G. juice, coconut aminos, avocado oil, sugar, salt, garlic powder, ginger and green onions. Pour the marinade over the chicken. Marinate the chicken in the refrigerator for a minimum of 6 hours, or overnight for optimal flavor.

Make Your Own P.O.G. Juice: If you can't find prepared P.O.G. juice, you can make your own by combining ¾ cup (180 ml) of passion fruit juice, ¾ cup (180 ml) of guava juice and ½ cup (120 ml) of orange juice.

(continued)

p.o.g. chicken on greens (cont.)

pineapple ranch dressing

1 cup (165 g) canned crushed pineapple, undrained

½ cup (120 ml) Back Porch Mayo (page 134)

½ cup (120 ml) plain unsweetened almond milk

½ (6-oz [168-g]) ripe avocado, roughly chopped

1½ tsp (9 g) fine sea salt

¼ tsp garlic powder

¼ tsp ground ginger

1 tsp black sesame seeds

1 green onion, finely chopped

1 tbsp (1 g) finely chopped fresh cilantro

greens

10 oz (280 g) romaine hearts, cut in half lengthwise

1 tsp fine sea salt

1 large Ataulfo mango, peeled and cut into bite-sized pieces

1 cup (165 g) fresh pineapple tidbits

1 (5-oz [140-g]) blood orange, cut into rings or segments

1 (6-oz [168-g]) avocado, thinly sliced

Garlic-Dill Pickled Onions (page 137), as needed

2 (1½-oz [42-g]) passion fruits, halved

Furikake or sesame seeds, as needed (optional)

3 green onions, thinly sliced

Finely chopped fresh cilantro, as needed (optional)

To make the pineapple ranch dressing, place the pineapple and its liquid, Back Porch Mayo, almond milk, avocado, salt, garlic powder and ginger in a narrow 2-cup (480-ml) Mason jar. Use an immersion blender to blend the ingredients until they are well combined and the pineapple and avocado are smooth. When the mixture is smooth, add the sesame seeds, green onion and cilantro, stirring them into the dressing to combine everything. Alternatively, you can place the ingredients in a food processor and pulse to combine them.

When you're ready to cook the chicken, remove it from the refrigerator and allow it to come to room temperature. Grill the chicken over medium-high heat on a stovetop grill pan or on an outdoor grill for 6 to 7 minutes, until its internal temperature reaches 165°F (74°C)—the exact cooking time will depend on the grill's temperature and the thickness of the chicken. Remove the chicken from the grill and transfer it to a cutting board. Allow the chicken to rest for at least 10 minutes while you prepare the greens.

To prepare the greens, arrange the romaine hearts on a large serving platter and sprinkle them with the salt.

Slice the chicken into ½-inch (1.3-cm)-thick strips and place them on the lettuce. Arrange the mango, pineapple, orange, avocado and our Garlic-Dill Pickled Onions around the chicken and greens. Place the passion fruits on the platter. Sprinkle everything with the furikake (if using), green onions and cilantro (if using). Serve the dish family style with the pineapple ranch on the side.

patsy's sloppy joes

This recipe is a beloved one that evokes warm, fuzzy food memories for many people in our family. The first time we saw our Patsy whip up this recipe, we were in awe. She originally made it with a canned condensed chicken gumbo soup, then simply seasoned it with ketchup, mustard and Worcestershire sauce. We've come up with what we think is a spectacular representation of her original: tasty ground beef swimming in a pseudo chicken gumbo and layers of subtly sweet flavors. We think once you toast up one of our Hamburger Buns (page 128) and smear on a layer of our Back Porch Mayo (page 134), you will wonder how you were ever satisfied with sloppy joes before.

yield: 4 cups (227 g) of sloppy joe filling

1 tbsp (15 ml) avocado oil

1 lb (454 g) grass-fed ground beef

½ cup (80 g) diced sweet onion

¼ cup (37 g) diced red bell pepper

1 tbsp (8 g) cassava flour

1¼ cups (300 ml) unsalted chicken bone broth

2 tbsp (32 g) tomato paste

1 tbsp (15 ml) apple cider vinegar

½ cup (97 g) diced frozen okra

1 tsp fine sea salt

¼ tsp dried thyme

⅛ tsp dried oregano

1 cup (240 ml) sugar-free ketchup

2 tbsp (30 ml) yellow mustard

2 tbsp (26 g) coconut sugar

4 tsp (20 ml) organic Worcestershire sauce

½ cup (93 g) cooked white basmati rice (optional; reduce the bone broth to 1 cup [240 ml] if not using)

Hamburger Buns (page 128), for serving (optional)

Back Porch Mayo (page 134), for serving (optional)

Heat a 10-inch (25-cm) cast-iron skillet over medium heat. Add the avocado oil, beef, onion and bell pepper. Cook the mixture for 8 to 10 minutes, stirring it occasionally, until the beef is no longer pink and the veggies are soft and slightly golden brown.

Sprinkle the cassava flour over the meat and stir to coat everything with the flour. Then add the bone broth, tomato paste, vinegar, okra, salt, thyme and oregano. Stir the mixture to combine the ingredients well. Bring the mixture to a gentle simmer, then reduce the heat to low and simmer the mixture for 5 to 7 minutes, stirring it occasionally. The cassava flour and okra will thicken the mixture at this point.

Add the ketchup, mustard, sugar, Worcestershire sauce and rice (if using) and stir to combine everything well. Simmer the mixture for 10 minutes, stirring it occasionally.

Toast the Hamburger Buns (if using). Spread the Back Porch Mayo (if using) on the bottom bun. Fill the bun with 4 to 5 tablespoons (60 to 75 g) of the warm filling. Top the filling with the other half of the bun.

creamy chicken soup over rice

There were many busy weeknights as a family of six when the only thing that we could get on the table was canned cream of chicken soup. Add some rice, and you've got a quick and easy meal to feed the many hungry mouths, all while being delicious! We aren't sure if you've looked at the ingredients for that soup lately, but they're not the best for the gut. We've re-created this canned soup to be dairy-free and even more delicious. Our version does take a bit longer to throw together than opening a can, but we think that extra effort is worth the wonderful flavor of this dish.

yield: 4 servings

1 tbsp (15 ml) avocado oil

1 small onion, diced

1½ cups (210 g) diced cooked chicken

½ lb (224 g) fresh asparagus spears, woody ends cut off and sliced into thirds

2½ tbsp (20 g) cassava flour

2 cups (480 ml) unsalted chicken bone broth

2 oz (56 g) dairy-free cream cheese

2 tbsp (30 ml) plain unsweetened almond milk

2 tsp (12 g) fine sea salt, plus additional as needed

2 tsp (6 g) garlic powder

Juice of ½ (2- to 3-oz [56- to 84-g]) lemon, plus additional as needed

½ tsp fish sauce

Black pepper, as needed

2 tbsp (8 g) roughly chopped fresh parsley (optional)

Lemon wedges, for serving (optional)

2 slices crispy prosciutto, for serving (optional)

Cooked white basmati rice, cauliflower rice or zoodles, for serving

Heat a 10-inch (25-cm) cast-iron skillet over medium heat. Add the avocado oil and heat it until it is shimmering. Add the onion and sauté it for 6 to 8 minutes, stirring it occasionally, until it is soft and golden brown.

Add the chicken and asparagus, stirring the mixture until everything is warmed through. Sprinkle the mixture with the cassava flour and stir it to coat everything with the flour. Cook the mixture for 1 minute.

Pour in the bone broth; add the cream cheese and almond milk. Cook the mixture for 5 to 7 minutes, stirring it occasionally, until the mixture is smooth and thick.

Add the salt, garlic powder, lemon juice, fish sauce and black pepper, stirring the ingredients to combine them. Taste the soup and add more salt or lemon juice if needed. Sprinkle the soup with the parsley (if using). Serve the soup with the lemon wedges (if using) and prosciutto (if using) over the rice (if you tolerate it), cauliflower rice or zoodles.

hawaiian haystacks

If you're on the hunt for a recipe that feeds a crowd, is customizable and is also delicious, we're happy to tell you that your search ends here! We've always served it over rice, but it would still be delightful on its own or over some cauliflower rice, potatoes, zoodles or whatever you prefer. It's plenty flavorful, so it goes best with a neutral base. No matter what you end up pairing it with, you're going to be happy to have some leftovers for the next day.

yield: 14 servings

4 (8-oz [224-g]) boneless, skinless chicken breasts

2 cups (480 ml) unsalted chicken bone broth, plus additional if needed

2½ cups (600 ml) canned or bottled pineapple juice, divided

¼ cup (60 ml) coconut aminos

1 tbsp (15 ml) fish sauce

1½ tsp (9 g) fine sea salt, plus additional if needed

1 tsp sesame oil

1½ tsp (5 g) black sesame seeds (optional)

¼ tsp garlic powder

¼ tsp ground ginger

¼ tsp black pepper

½ cup (74 g) sliced water chestnuts

½ cup (50 g) thinly sliced green onions

½ cup (120 ml) coconut milk or nut milk of choice

6 tbsp (48 g) cassava flour

1 small bunch fresh cilantro, finely chopped (optional)

Toppings of choice (see sidebar)

Place the chicken breasts in a 6- to 8-quart (5.8- to 7.8-L) slow cooker. Pour in the bone broth, 2 cups (480 ml) of the pineapple juice, coconut aminos, fish sauce, salt and sesame oil. Stir the mixture to combine everything and cook the chicken on high for 6 hours. The chicken should be starting to fall apart; if not, cook it for 1 more hour.

Transfer the chicken to a cutting board, allow it to cool slightly and then shred it with two forks. Set the chicken aside.

Pour the liquid from the slow cooker through a fine-mesh sieve into a 6-quart (5.8-L) stockpot and place it over medium heat. Add the additional bone broth, if needed, to equal 4 cups (960 ml) of liquid. Add the sesame seeds (if using), garlic powder, ginger, black pepper, water chestnuts and green onions, stirring the ingredients well to combine them. Bring this mixture to a slow boil.

In a small bowl, combine the remaining ½ cup (120 ml) of pineapple juice and the coconut milk. Whisk in the cassava flour until you have a smooth slurry. While whisking the hot chicken broth mixture in the stockpot, slowly pour in the slurry. The broth mixture will thicken up. Add the shredded chicken and cilantro (if using) and stir to combine everything. Taste the soup and add more salt if needed.

Serve the soup over rice, cauliflower rice, warmed zoodles, glass noodles or as is with the toppings of your choice.

A Few of Our Favorite Toppings: We love topping the soup with diced ham, pineapple chunks, sliced almonds, diced red bell peppers, finely diced red onion, sliced olives, sliced green onions, coconut flakes, sliced mushrooms, diced tomatoes, gluten-free crunchy chow mein noodles and coconut aminos. The possibilities are endless.

Instant Pot Instructions: Add the chicken to the Instant Pot and add only 1 cup (240 ml) of the chicken bone broth and 1 cup (240 ml) of the pineapple juice. Cook the mixture at high pressure for 8 to 10 minutes for fresh chicken breast or for 10 to 12 minutes for frozen chicken. Then follow the directions in the recipe, adding the remaining bone broth and pineapple juice when you add the sesame seeds (if using), garlic powder, ginger, black pepper, water chestnuts and green onions. Follow the remaining steps of the recipe as directed.

cottage pie

We learned something new when we were doing research for this recipe. Did you know that the name "shepherd's pie" applies only when you use lamb? If you're using ground beef, as we have here, it's called cottage pie. So when we've enjoyed this over the years, we definitely used the wrong name—but we have loved it regardless. A layer of creamy mashed potatoes covering a flavorful gravy loaded with soft veggies and savory beef brings comfort in every single bite.

yield: 8 servings

mashed potatoes

2½ tsp (15 g) fine sea salt, divided

1½ lb (681 g) russet potatoes, peeled and cut into 1" (2.5-cm) cubes

4 to 6 tbsp (60 to 90 ml) plain unsweetened almond milk

3 to 4 tbsp (36 to 48 g) ghee

To make the mashed potatoes, fill a 3-quart (2.9-L) pot with cold water and then add 2 teaspoons (12 g) of the salt. Place the potatoes in the cold water. Cover the pot, set it over medium-high heat and bring the potatoes to a boil. Uncover the pot, reduce the heat to medium-low and maintain a simmer. Cook the potatoes for 10 to 15 minutes, until they are fork-tender and smash easily.

Drain the potatoes, then return them to the pot. Add 4 tablespoons (60 ml) of the almond milk, the ghee and the remaining ½ teaspoon of salt. Use a potato masher to mash the potatoes until they are smooth— if you prefer smoother potatoes, add the remaining 2 tablespoons (30 ml) of almond milk, 1 tablespoon (15 ml) at a time, and mash the potatoes until they reach your desired consistency. Set the mashed potatoes aside.

Preheat the oven to 400°F (204°C). Line a medium baking sheet with parchment paper.

(continued)

cottage pie (cont.)

filling

1 tbsp (15 ml) avocado oil

1 cup (160 g) diced onion

2 medium carrots, peeled and cut into 1" (2.5-cm) matchsticks

2 cloves garlic, minced

1 lb (454 g) grass-fed ground beef

1½ tsp (9 g) fine sea salt

3 tbsp (24 g) cassava flour

1 cup (240 ml) unsalted chicken bone broth

3 tbsp (45 ml) sugar-free ketchup

2 tbsp (30 ml) plain unsweetened almond milk

2 tsp (10 ml) balsamic vinegar

2 tsp (10 ml) organic Worcestershire sauce

1 tbsp (2 g) finely chopped fresh rosemary

¼ tsp porcini mushroom powder (page 162)

1 cup (134 g) frozen peas

1 cup (70 g) diced cremini mushrooms

3 pieces cooked bacon, roughly chopped

Finely chopped fresh parsley, as needed (optional)

To make the filling, warm a 10-inch (25-cm) cast-iron skillet over medium heat. Add the avocado oil and allow it to warm. Add the onion and the carrots and sauté them for 5 to 7 minutes, until they are soft and becoming golden brown along the edges. Add the garlic, stirring to combine the ingredients, and cook the mixture for 40 to 60 seconds, until the garlic is fragrant. Add the ground beef and salt and cook it for 10 to 12 minutes, stirring the mixture occasionally, until the beef is no longer pink. Sprinkle the cassava flour over the meat mixture and stir to coat it with the flour. Cook the mixture for about 1 minute. Pour in the bone broth, ketchup, almond milk, balsamic vinegar, Worcestershire sauce, rosemary and porcini mushroom powder, stirring to combine them with the meat mixture. Bring the mixture to a gentle simmer, then reduce the heat to low and cook it for 2 to 4 minutes, stirring it occasionally, until the sauce thickens. Add the peas, cremini mushrooms and bacon and stir the ingredients until everything is well combined. Smooth the top of the mixture evenly in the skillet and remove it from the heat.

Using a spoon, place the mashed potatoes on top of the filling, being sure to start around the edges—this creates a seal to prevent the filling from bubbling up. Spread out the potatoes carefully, then use a fork to create a pattern on top of the potatoes. This will create lovely crisp peaks that will take on a hint of golden-brown color as the cottage pie bakes.

Place the cottage pie on the prepared baking sheet and bake it for 30 minutes, or just until the potatoes begin to brown. Remove the cottage pie from the oven and let it rest for about 15 minutes before serving it. Garnish with fresh parsley, if desired.

Store any leftovers in an airtight container in the refrigerator for 4 to 5 days.

instant pot® mini sirloin burger soup

Here's a blast from the past that's been brought back to our table. Our family has enjoyed the canned variety of mini sirloin burger soup for three generations. When we changed our diet, we had to forfeit enjoying this family favorite—until now! The mini burgers in this recipe are tender and so flavorful. The potatoes, carrots and other veggies are utterly delicious, all swimming in a tasty gravy. In our opinion, this recipe rivals the canned soup and is so much better for our health. Packed with real ingredients and zero junk, this is a simple meal that has all those comfort-flavor notes and brings us fond memories. Sitting around the table after a long day of school and work, we can decompress over this warm meal. We like to serve this soup over basmati rice, but it is also lovely over mashed potatoes, cauliflower rice, zoodles or swoodles.

yield: **8 servings**

mini burgers

1 lb (454 g) grass-fed ground beef

2 tbsp (16 g) cassava flour

2 tsp (4 g) mustard powder

2 tsp (10 ml) apple cider vinegar

¾ tsp fine sea salt

½ tsp onion powder

¼ tsp porcini mushroom powder (page 162)

1 large egg, at room temperature

Avocado oil, as needed

Prepare a 13 x 18–inch (33 x 45–cm) baking sheet by lining it with plastic wrap.

To make the mini burgers, place the ground beef, cassava flour, mustard powder, apple cider vinegar, salt, onion powder, mushroom powder and egg in a medium bowl. For the best results, combine the ingredients using your hands—but if that isn't for you, use a wooden spoon or spatula. Mix the ingredients together until they are fully incorporated.

Shape 1 tablespoon (15 g) of the burger mixture into a small oval patty. Place the patty on the prepared baking sheet. Repeat this process with the remaining burger mixture. You should have about 30 small patties.

Preheat a 10- to 12-inch (25- to 30-cm) cast-iron skillet or a stovetop grill pan over medium heat. If you are using a skillet, warm a bit of the avocado oil in the skillet. Working in batches, cook the patties for 2 to 4 minutes per side, until they have a golden sear or grill marks. Transfer the cooked patties to a medium bowl. Repeat this process with the remaining patties.

(continued)

instant pot® mini sirloin burger soup (cont.)

soup

2 large russet potatoes, peeled and cut into ½" (1.3-cm) cubes

2 large carrots, peeled and sliced into ½" (1.3-cm)-thick rounds

4 cups (960 ml) unsalted chicken bone broth

¼ cup (60 ml) sugar-free ketchup

1 tsp fine sea salt

3 tbsp (24 g) cassava flour

½ cup (120 ml) plain unsweetened almond milk

1 cup (134 g) frozen peas

1 cup (110 g) 1" (2.5 cm)-long fresh or frozen green beans

¼ cup (60 ml) Mango Steak Sauce (page 149)

1 tbsp (15 ml) balsamic vinegar

1 tbsp (15 ml) coconut aminos

Finely chopped fresh parsley, as needed (optional)

To make the soup, combine the potatoes, carrots, bone broth, ketchup and salt in the insert of a 6-quart (5.8-L) Instant Pot. Stir the ingredients to combine them, then secure the Instant Pot's lid in place. Cook the vegetable mixture at high pressure for 8 minutes, and then manually release the pressure.

In a small bowl, mix together the cassava flour and almond milk to make a smooth slurry. Pour the slurry into the hot vegetable mixture, stirring to combine everything. Add the peas, green beans, Mango Steak Sauce, balsamic vinegar, coconut aminos and the cooked mini burgers. Stir the ingredients to combine them and secure the Instant Pot's lid in place. Cook the soup at high pressure for 3 minutes. Manually release the pressure. Stir in the parsley (if using) and serve the soup.

dilly crusted salmon

When you're looking for an unbelievably easy meal to get on the table quickly, salmon is a perfect protein. We enjoy seafood, but since we don't live in an area where wild-caught seafood is readily available, we do our best to purchase sustainably-sourced frozen seafood when we can. We've paired these wild-caught fillets with the classic flavors of lemon and dill. To add another layer of flavor and texture, we've topped the salmon with crunchy, freshly seasoned pork panko. Since the salmon bakes so quickly, you'll have just enough time to prepare a side like our Simple and Quick Wedge Salad (page 93). Dinner is ready in a jiffy!

yield: 4 servings

4 (6- to 8-oz [168- to 224-g])
wild-caught skinless or skin-on
salmon fillets
½ tsp fine sea salt, divided
2 tbsp (30 ml) Back Porch Mayo
(page 134)
⅓ cup (19 g) pork panko
1½ tsp (2 g) finely chopped fresh dill,
divided, plus additional as needed
½ tsp garlic powder
½ tsp dried chives
Lemon wedges, for serving

Preheat the oven to 415°F (213°C). Prepare a 13 x 18–inch (33 x 45–cm) baking sheet by lining it with parchment paper. Place the salmon fillets on a plate lined with paper towels and pat them dry with more paper towels. Sprinkle the fillets with ¼ teaspoon of the salt. Let them come to room temperature.

Place the dried fillets on the prepared baking sheet. Spread about ½ tablespoon (8 ml) of the Back Porch Mayo on top of each fillet.

In a small bowl, combine the pork panko, 1 teaspoon of the dill, garlic powder, dried chives and remaining ¼ teaspoon of the salt. Toss the ingredients to combine them. Sprinkle the pork panko mixture evenly over the top of each fillet, pressing the mixture down slightly to adhere it to the fish.

Bake the salmon for 6 to 8 minutes, until it is flaky and light pink. Remove the fillets from the oven and serve them with the lemon wedges and additional dill.

comforting and creamy chicken 'n' dumplings

When we polled our followers on Instagram for their favorite comfort foods, chicken and dumplings was a resounding favorite. We completely understand. The creamy soup and a bounty of tender veggies with dumplings nestled on top of it all is difficult not to love. When Michelle enjoyed this meal growing up, the dumplings were made with that boxed biscuit mix. No shame—it's what everyone did, and they were pretty tasty. For our recipe, we make the dumplings using the biscuits from our Biscuits 'n' Gravy (page 23). Winner, winner, chicken dinner! Don't skip using bone-in, skin-on chicken in the soup. The deep flavor it adds to the soup stock is essential. This recipe takes some time and attention, but you will not be disappointed; it's worth every minute.

yield: 8 servings

soup

2½ lb (1.1 kg) bone-in, skin-on chicken breasts and thighs

2 tsp (12 g) kosher salt

2 medium ribs celery

4 medium carrots, divided

1 medium sweet onion

1 head garlic

2 tsp (6 g) black peppercorns

½ oz (14 g) fresh dill, divided, plus additional for garnishing

¼ cup (7 g) dried porcini mushrooms

7 cups (1.7 L) unsalted chicken bone broth

To prepare the soup, pat the chicken dry with paper towels, then sprinkle the kosher salt on all the chicken pieces and rub it into the meat; set aside.

Prepare the vegetables for the soup base. Coarsely chop the celery. Peel the carrots and coarsely chop 2 of them; set the remaining 2 carrots aside. Cut the onion into quarters, leaving the skin on the quarters for flavor. Cut the head of garlic in half crosswise, leaving the skin on it as well.

Place the chicken, cut veggies, peppercorns, ¼ ounce (7 g) of the dill and porcini mushrooms in an 8-quart (1.9-L) stockpot. Cover them with the bone broth and bring the mixture to a simmer over medium-high heat. Reduce the heat to medium-low to maintain a gentle simmer. Use a large spoon to skim off any foam that may gather on the surface. Cook the mixture for 20 to 25 minutes, or until the internal temperature of the chicken's thickest part reaches 155°F (68°C).

1 cup (110 g) 1" (2.5)-long fresh or frozen green beans

½ cup (67 g) frozen peas

1 tsp roughly chopped fresh thyme

1½ tsp (9 g) fine sea salt (optional)

Black pepper, as needed

¼ cup (33 g) cassava flour

½ cup (120 ml) plain unsweetened almond milk

dumplings

1 uncooked recipe biscuits (page 23)

½ tsp finely chopped fresh dill (optional)

½ tsp fine sea salt

While the soup base cooks, prepare the dumplings. Prepare our biscuit recipe on page 23, but add the dill (if using) and salt to the recipe—there is no need to roll out the dough. Set the dough aside while the soup continues to cook.

Using tongs, carefully lift the chicken pieces out of the stockpot and transfer them to a cutting board. Let them rest until they are cool enough to handle. Continue to simmer the soup base for approximately 10 minutes, until it has reduced by 1 to 2 inches (2.5 to 5 cm). Meanwhile, debone the chicken, discard the bones and shred the chicken into bite-sized pieces.

Place a fine-mesh sieve over a 5-quart (1.2-L) stockpot. Strain the soup base into the stockpot and discard the solids. Cut the 2 remaining carrots into ½-inch (1.3-cm) pieces and finely chop the remaining ¼ ounce (7 g) of the dill. Add the chicken, carrots, green beans, peas and thyme to the broth and cook them over medium-low heat for 4 to 5 minutes, until the vegetables are tender. Taste the broth and add the fine sea salt (if needed), black pepper and the chopped dill.

To thicken the soup, mix together the cassava flour and almond milk in a small bowl until they create a smooth slurry. While stirring the soup, pour the slurry into the soup and stir to combine everything. The soup will thicken as it warms.

While the soup is simmering over medium-low heat, drop 1 tablespoon (15 g) of the dumpling dough at a time into the soup, arranging them around the soup's surface as you add them. Cover the pot and cook the chicken and dumplings for about 10 minutes. Remove a dumpling and split it with a fork. The dumplings are done when the centers are cooked through and fluffy.

Serve the chicken and dumplings by ladling it into individual bowls and garnishing each serving with additional chopped dill.

*See image on page 40.

creamy mushroom poutine

One of our favorite family traditions is the dinners we make to celebrate the culture and food of the country hosting the Olympics. When our Canadian neighbors hosted the Winter Olympics in 2010, we were smitten with their poutine. Potatoes and gravy? Heaven. While poutine is traditionally served with cheese curds, we had to change that aspect of the recipe to keep our bellies happy. We decided on a delicious mushroom gravy in our version and topped it with dollops of dairy-free sour cream. It's one of the many fun meals we've enjoyed while watching the Olympics over the years.

yield: 4 servings

fries

2 lb (908 g) russet potatoes, peeled and cut into ¼" (6-mm)-thick fries

2 tbsp (30 ml) avocado oil

2 tsp (12 g) fine sea salt, divided

1 tsp finely chopped fresh parsley (optional)

mushroom gravy

1½ tsp (8 ml) avocado oil

3 oz (84 g) cremini mushrooms, cleaned and sliced into ½" (1.3-cm)-thick pieces

1½ tbsp (12 g) cassava flour

½ tsp fine sea salt

1 cup (240 ml) unsalted chicken bone broth

1 tbsp (15 ml) balsamic vinegar

½ tbsp (1 g) finely chopped fresh thyme

1 tsp grass-fed butter or ghee

4 tbsp (60 ml) dairy-free sour cream, divided

1 tbsp (15 ml) fresh lemon juice

1½ tsp (8 ml) coconut aminos

Preheat the oven to 415°F (213°C).

To make the fries, place the potatoes in a large bowl of water and refrigerate them for 1 hour. Drain the potatoes and cover them with hot tap water. Let them soak in the hot water for 10 minutes. Drain the potatoes again and lay the fries out on a layer of paper towels. Pat them dry with the paper towels and wipe out and dry the bowl.

Transfer the fries to the dry bowl and drizzle them with the avocado oil and 1½ teaspoons (9 g) of the salt. Divide the fries between two 13 x 18–inch (33 x 45–cm) baking sheets, being sure to arrange them in a single layer. Bake the fries for 30 to 40 minutes, or until they're golden and crispy.

While the fries bake, prepare the mushroom gravy. Heat a 10-inch (25-cm) cast-iron skillet over medium heat. Add the avocado oil and mushrooms, tossing the mushrooms to coat them in the oil. Cook them for 8 to 10 minutes, stirring them occasionally, until they are golden brown. Sprinkle the cassava flour over the mushrooms and stir to coat them with the flour.

Add the salt and bone broth and stir the mixture—it should begin to thicken up. Add the balsamic vinegar, thyme, butter, 1 tablespoon (15 ml) of the sour cream, lemon juice and coconut aminos. Stir the mixture to combine all of the ingredients.

To serve the poutine, place the fries on a large platter and sprinkle them with the remaining ½ teaspoon of salt. Drizzle about half of the gravy over the fries and serve the rest in a small vessel on the platter. Add dollops of the remaining 3 tablespoons (45 ml) of sour cream and sprinkle the poutine with the parsley (if using).

1 cup (110 g) 1" (2.5)-long fresh or frozen green beans
½ cup (67 g) frozen peas
1 tsp roughly chopped fresh thyme
1½ tsp (9 g) fine sea salt (optional)
Black pepper, as needed
¼ cup (33 g) cassava flour
½ cup (120 ml) plain unsweetened almond milk

dumplings

1 uncooked recipe biscuits (page 23)
½ tsp finely chopped fresh dill (optional)
½ tsp fine sea salt

While the soup base cooks, prepare the dumplings. Prepare our biscuit recipe on page 23, but add the dill (if using) and salt to the recipe—there is no need to roll out the dough. Set the dough aside while the soup continues to cook.

Using tongs, carefully lift the chicken pieces out of the stockpot and transfer them to a cutting board. Let them rest until they are cool enough to handle. Continue to simmer the soup base for approximately 10 minutes, until it has reduced by 1 to 2 inches (2.5 to 5 cm). Meanwhile, debone the chicken, discard the bones and shred the chicken into bite-sized pieces.

Place a fine-mesh sieve over a 5-quart (1.2-L) stockpot. Strain the soup base into the stockpot and discard the solids. Cut the 2 remaining carrots into ½-inch (1.3-cm) pieces and finely chop the remaining ¼ ounce (7 g) of the dill. Add the chicken, carrots, green beans, peas and thyme to the broth and cook them over medium-low heat for 4 to 5 minutes, until the vegetables are tender. Taste the broth and add the fine sea salt (if needed), black pepper and the chopped dill.

To thicken the soup, mix together the cassava flour and almond milk in a small bowl until they create a smooth slurry. While stirring the soup, pour the slurry into the soup and stir to combine everything. The soup will thicken as it warms.

While the soup is simmering over medium-low heat, drop 1 tablespoon (15 g) of the dumpling dough at a time into the soup, arranging them around the soup's surface as you add them. Cover the pot and cook the chicken and dumplings for about 10 minutes. Remove a dumpling and split it with a fork. The dumplings are done when the centers are cooked through and fluffy.

Serve the chicken and dumplings by ladling it into individual bowls and garnishing each serving with additional chopped dill.

*See image on page 40.

lil' nibbles

It might be a Utah thing, but we've found ourselves invited to countless potluck-style barbecues over the years. At these events, we see a lot of the same things over and over again, and we'll be honest: A lot of them aren't entirely appetizing or Paleo-friendly! We took it upon ourselves to make sure there was at least one delicious and better-for-you side at these events, and we think we did a pretty dang good job. Many people sneak up to us after these events to ask for the recipes, and to be honest, we can't blame them. Dishes like these deserve to be shared and enjoyed by everyone.

You'll find a common flavor theme here, and that is "zesty!" We love that little zing we get in our mouths when we have something vinegary, and we think these sides are absolutely mouthwatering. Just because these are side dishes doesn't mean they don't deserve the spotlight. Many of the recipes here are packed full of vegetables! And then you'll find others, like Honey Graham Crackers (page 86) and Dill Pickle Roll-Ups (page 89), that are small snacks we could not leave out. We suspect you'll struggle to keep leftovers of these recipes, because every single one is exceptionally delicious.

pesto potato salad

We love potatoes in all their glorious forms and preparations: baked, fried, roasted, in soups or in a salad. The tasty possibilities are endless. The russets used in this recipe are baked in cubes and bathed in our Toasted Pine Nut Arugula Pesto (page 138) while they're warm, then they're tossed with a few other simple ingredients. This is a delicious warm potato salad, filled with layers of texture and unique flavors. It's perfect for a quick addition to lunch—or you can double the recipe and serve it as a healthy side dish with dinner.

yield: **2 servings**

2 pieces prosciutto

2 cups (280 g) peeled russet potatoes, cubed into 1" (2.5-cm) pieces

1½ tsp (8 ml) avocado oil

½ tsp fine sea salt

1 tbsp (15 ml) Toasted Pine Nut Arugula Pesto (page 138)

1 tbsp (8 g) toasted pine nuts (optional)

¼ cup (5 g) arugula (optional)

To bake the prosciutto in an air fryer, line the baking sheet insert with parchment paper. Place the prosciutto on the prepared baking sheet insert. Air-fry the prosciutto at 400°F (204°C) for approximately 10 minutes, or until it is curled up and crispy. Transfer the prosciutto to a paper towel and set it aside.

To bake the prosciutto in the oven, preheat the oven to 350°F (177°C). Line a 13 x 18–inch (33 x 45–cm) baking sheet with parchment paper. Place the prosciutto on the prepared baking sheet and bake it for 10 to 12 minutes, or until it is curled up and crispy.

Place the potatoes in a small bowl and toss them with the avocado oil and salt. Transfer them to the air fryer basket and air-fry them at 400°F (204°C) for 10 to 12 minutes, or until they are golden brown.

Transfer the potatoes to a medium bowl and top them with the Toasted Pine Nut Arugula Pesto. Gently stir the potatoes to coat them with the pesto. Crumble the prosciutto on top of the potatoes, then add the pine nuts (if using) and arugula (if using) and toss the potato salad again. Serve while it's warm.

broccoli-bacon picnic salad

This little salad is umami-packed! It's one of our all-time family favorites and was requested for many of our gatherings even before we began our Paleo lifestyle. It's loaded with an abundance of fresh broccoli, tomatoes and crispy bacon, giving you all the textures and flavors you could ask for in a side dish. The dressing is simple and yet so tasty, accenting the flavors of the ingredients perfectly.

yield: 6 servings

¼ cup (34 g) pine nuts, plus additional as needed

4 cups (364 g) bite-sized fresh broccoli florets

1 cup (149 g) halved or quartered grape tomatoes

1 cup (224 g) roughly chopped cooked bacon, plus additional as needed

¼ cup (40 g) diced red onion

½ cup (120 ml) Back Porch Mayo (page 134)

2 tsp (10 ml) red wine vinegar

1 tsp (6 g) fine sea salt

½ tsp Dijon mustard

¼ tsp black pepper

Place the pine nuts in a dry small skillet over low heat and toast them for 5 to 7 minutes, until they're golden. Keep a close eye on them, as they can go from golden to burnt quickly.

In a large bowl, combine the broccoli, tomatoes, bacon, onion and pine nuts. Set the bowl aside.

In a small bowl, whisk together the Back Porch Mayo, red wine vinegar, salt, mustard and black pepper until the dressing is smooth.

Pour the dressing over the broccoli mixture and gently toss the salad to coat it with the dressing.

Serve the salad immediately with additional pine nuts or bacon. Or store the salad in the refrigerator until you are ready to serve it. This salad is best enjoyed the day it's made. Store the leftovers in the refrigerator and serve them within 2 days for optimal freshness.

zesty pasta salad

Do you have a summer barbecue coming up? Or maybe a spring picnic? Look no further for what to make, because this zesty pasta salad is about to be the talk of the town at your get-together. The red wine vinegar brightens up all the vegetables in this dish. This pasta salad is an easy side that's been the star at many summer evening meals for our family, and Makenna has been known to steal some dressing-covered noodles before the salad has made it to the table. We suspect you might have the same problem, as this salad is dang delicious.

yield: **6 servings**

¼ cup (60 ml) red wine vinegar

1 tbsp (9 g) sesame seeds

2 tsp (2 g) dried oregano

2 tsp (4 g) paprika

1½ tsp (9 g) fine sea salt

1 tsp garlic powder

½ tsp ground celery seeds

½ tsp black pepper

¾ cup (180 ml) avocado oil

¾ cup (75 g) thinly sliced green onions

1 cup (149 g) grape tomatoes, cut in half

4 oz (112 g) cassava-flour spiral pasta

5 oz (140 g) mini cucumbers, cut into bite-sized pieces

7 oz (196 g) hearts of palm, drained and sliced into ½" (1.3-cm)-thick rings

3 oz (84 g) cremini mushrooms, cleaned and thinly sliced

2 oz (56 g) black olives, thinly sliced

2 oz (56 g) salami, cut into bite-sized pieces

In a small bowl, whisk together the red wine vinegar, sesame seeds, oregano, paprika, salt, garlic powder, ground celery seeds and black pepper. Slowly pour in the avocado oil in a thin stream, whisking the mixture constantly, until the dressing is emulsified. Set the dressing aside.

In medium bowl, combine the green onions and the tomatoes. Pour three-fourths of the dressing into this bowl and stir to combine the ingredients. For optimal flavor, let this mixture marinate for about 30 minutes.

When you are ready to assemble the salad, prepare the pasta according to the package's directions, being careful not to overcook it. The pasta should be just al dente, with a bit of bite. Once the pasta is ready, drain it in a colander and run cool water over it. Drain the rinsed pasta well.

Transfer the pasta to the desired serving bowl. Add the cucumbers, hearts of palm, mushrooms, olives and salami. Pour the tomato–green onion mixture over the top and gently stir the salad to coat all the pasta and veggies with dressing. Taste the veggies and add more dressing and/or salt if desired, stirring to coat everything. When you are ready to serve the salad, transfer it to a medium bowl. This salad is best enjoyed the day you make it, but it can be stored in the refrigerator for up to 3 days.

crispy zucchini fries

These zucchini fries were on repeat when the kids would run home for lunch with a gaggle of friends during high school and were also enjoyed as a great side dish with dinner. We often had to make several batches to feed the masses. These zucchini fries are coated with pork panko and potato flakes, and when they bake, the coating becomes crunchy and golden. They're finger food at its finest, and they're made even better when they're served with our Creamy Sweet Onion Dip (page 145). We think you'll love this healthy and fresh rendition of the classic French fry.

yield: **3 servings**

2 medium zucchini about 2½"
(6 cm) in diameter

¼ cup (33 g) cassava flour

1 large egg, at room temperature

½ cup (28 g) pork panko

½ cup (30 g) potato flakes

1 tsp dried parsley

½ tsp fine sea salt

½ tsp garlic powder

Finely chopped fresh parsley, for garnishing (optional)

1 recipe Creamy Sweet Onion Dip (page 145), for serving

Slice the zucchini into quarters lengthwise and discard the ends. Carefully remove the seeds, then cut each quarter into approximately 2½-inch (6-cm) lengths. Lay the zucchini pieces on a paper towel and pat them dry.

Prepare your coating station. Place the cassava flour in a shallow bowl, and then set it aside. Whisk the egg in a second shallow bowl. In a third shallow bowl, combine the pork panko, potato flakes, dried parsley, salt and garlic powder, tossing to incorporate the ingredients.

If you will be baking the zucchini fries, preheat the oven to 425°F (218°C). Line a 13 x 18–inch (33 x 45–cm) baking sheet with parchment paper. If you will be air-frying the fries, spray with avocado oil if suggested by your air-fryer manufacturer.

To coat the fries, dip two to three fries at a time into the flour, coating them and shaking off the excess. Then dip the fries into the egg, allowing the excess to drip off. Then dip the fries into the panko mixture. Rotate the fries to coat them in the panko mixture, then place them on the prepared baking sheet or in the air fryer basket. Repeat this process until all the zucchini fries are coated. Don't be tempted to do too many zucchini fries at once—two or three at a time works best.

If you are baking the fries in the oven, place the fries on the baking sheet and bake for 13 to 15 minutes, or until the edges are golden and crispy. If you are air-frying the fries, place the basket in the air fryer and air-fry the fries at 400°F (204°C) for 8 to 10 minutes, or until the edges are golden and crispy.

Transfer the zucchini fries to a serving platter, garnish them with the fresh parsley (if using) and serve them with the Creamy Sweet Onion Dip.

honey graham crackers

Everyone loves graham crackers. They're great with milk, they can be used to make pie crusts and they can be turned into s'mores and frosting-filled cookies. Makenna in particular has childhood memories of eating graham crackers with milk while watching cartoons—which, to be clear, we don't necessarily advise, but they're just simple, delicious and really that good. This Paleo rendition is so versatile, making them a must-have in the pantry, and we think you'll absolutely love them.

yield: 18 to 20 crackers

¾ cup (100 g) plus 2 tbsp (16 g) cassava flour, plus additional as needed

3 tbsp (21 g) ground golden flaxseed

⅓ cup (63 g) maple sugar

¼ tsp kosher salt

¼ tsp baking powder

¼ tsp baking soda

7 tbsp (84 g) ghee

2 tbsp (30 ml) plain unsweetened almond milk

1 tbsp (15 ml) raw honey

½ tsp pure vanilla extract

Preheat the oven to 350°F (177°C) and line two 13 x 18–inch (33 x 45–cm) baking sheets with parchment paper.

In a medium bowl, combine the cassava flour, flaxseed, maple sugar, salt, baking powder and baking soda. Fluff the ingredients with a fork to combine them thoroughly. For the best results, use your fingers to incorporate the ghee into the flour mixture. Alternatively, you can use a small wooden spoon or spatula.

In a small bowl, whisk together the almond milk, honey and vanilla until they are smooth. Add the milk mixture to the flour mixture and mix the two until the dough comes together. Divide the dough in half and place one-half back in the bowl, covering it with plastic.

Grab two pieces of 13 x 18–inch (33 x 45–cm) parchment paper. Lightly dust one sheet with cassava flour, then place the first half of the dough onto this piece, lightly dusting the dough with more flour. Lay the second sheet on top and roll out to approximately ¼ inch (6 mm) thick. Cut the dough into 2½ x 2½–inch (6 x 6–cm) squares. Transfer the squares to one of the prepared baking sheets, placing the squares about 1 inch (2.5 cm) apart. Gather the dough scraps and reroll them until all the dough is used. Repeat this process with the other half of the dough.

Before baking the graham crackers, you can optionally give them the "graham cracker look" by scoring down the middle of each cracker with a knife, being careful not to cut all the way through. Then add six holes per half using the pointed end of a chopstick. Bake the graham crackers for 10 to 12 minutes, or until the edges begin to turn brown. Remove the graham crackers from the oven and let them cool on the baking sheets.

Store the graham crackers in an airtight container at room temperature for up to 1 week.

dill pickle roll-ups

Dill pickle roll-ups were a staple throughout Makenna's childhood and have continued to be just that for us both over the years. They're simple, creamy, tangy and delicious. Not to mention that the majority of the ingredients are usually refrigerator staples, making them an easy snack when you're not sure what to eat. You can dress them up by adding more veggies or dress them down by simplifying the ingredients to just turkey, cream cheese and pickles. No matter how you slice it, we think you're going to love them!

yield: 3 rolls

6 slices deli turkey

3 tbsp (45 g) dairy-free cream cheese

3 leaves red lettuce

1 tbsp (15 ml) Mustard Vinaigrette (page 146)

3 baby dill pickles

3 fresh chives

Lay 2 slices of deli turkey flat on a clean work surface, overlapping the ends. Then, repeat with the remaining 4 slices, so you have 3 groups of 2 overlapping slices.

Working assembly line–style, spread the cream cheese on the turkey. Then top the cream cheese with 1 lettuce leaf per turkey roll and a drizzle of the Mustard Vinaigrette.

Finally, place 1 pickle per two slices of turkey on the far edge and roll up the ingredients. Wrap a chive around the wrap and carefully tie it into a knot. Alternatively, you can secure the roll-ups with toothpicks through the center, or you can even slice and serve the roll-ups.

We recommend eating these roll-ups within 3 to 4 hours of making them.

grilled veggie platter

This platter is hands down the most-requested side dish for our summer feasts. The veggies gain spectacularly deep flavors from marinating all day, so be sure not to skip that step. We enjoy serving this family style so everyone can grab their favorite veggies. If you prefer different veggies, definitely give your favorites a dunk in this marinade instead. Plus, when you drain the veggies, you can put the marinade back in the jar and store it in the fridge for your next summer feast. We can almost guarantee this recipe is going to be your new go-to crowd-pleaser.

yield: 6 servings

2 (4 to 6" [10- to 15-cm]-diameter) portobello mushrooms

2 medium red onions

1 medium zucchini

1 (8-oz [224-g]) red bell pepper

½ lb (227 g) thin asparagus spears

2 recipes Balsamic Mason Jar Marinade (page 141)

Toasted Pine Nut Arugula Pesto (page 138), as needed (optional)

Roughly chopped fresh thyme, as needed (optional)

Clean the mushrooms and remove their stems. Slice the mushrooms into 1½-inch (4-cm)-thick sections or leave them whole. Peel the skin from the onions and slice them into ½-inch (1.3-cm)-thick rings. Slice the zucchini lengthwise into ¼-inch (6-mm)-thick pieces. Cut the stem and the seeds from the bell pepper, then slice it into quarters. Trim the woody ends from the asparagus.

Place the veggies in a 2-gallon (7.7-L) ziplock bag or a large glass baking dish, being careful to keep the onions in their ring shape so they're easier to grill. Pour the Balsamic Mason Jar Marinade over the veggies and let them marinate at room temperature for 6 to 8 hours. When you're ready to grill the veggies, drain the marinade back into the Mason jar and save it for another use.

Grill the veggies—in batches, if necessary—on an outdoor grill according to the manufacturer's directions or on an indoor stovetop grill pan over medium-high heat. Grill the veggies to your personal preference, but grill veggies together that require similar cooking times. For example, the onions and the bell peppers often take the longest and the asparagus will be the quickest. Ultimately, you should see some nice grill marks and the veggies should soften but not become mushy.

As the veggies finish grilling, lay them on a serving platter, arranging them as desired. Once all the veggies are grilled and on the serving platter, brush or spoon the pesto (if using) onto the veggies and sprinkle them with the thyme (if using), and then serve the platter. This dish is best served at room temperature.

simple and quick wedge salad

Is there anything better than a lovely wedge salad? While this is certainly not the traditional version, it's been our go-to for years thanks to the availability of artisan romaine lettuce. These fun heads of lettuce are like a cross between iceberg and romaine, full of crunch and with subtly sweet undertones. A great bonus: Since these halved beauties lie flat on your plate, the toppings don't roll off like they do with a classic wedge salad. Be sure to salt your greens before adding the dressing and toppings—trust us on this. We learned this technique from our friend Teri, and now we will never *not* salt our greens.

yield: **4 servings**

2 heads artisan romaine lettuce, halved lengthwise

¼ tsp fine sea salt

¼ cup (60 ml) Mustard Vinaigrette (page 146)

2 tbsp (30 ml) Back Porch Mayo (page 134)

½ cup (75 g) grape tomatoes, halved or quartered

2 tsp (2 g) finely chopped fresh chives

4 pieces crispy prosciutto, roughly chopped

Garlic-Dill Pickled Onions (page 137), as needed

Balsamic reduction (page 162), as needed (optional)

Lay the halves of romaine lettuce on a serving platter and season them with the salt.

In a small bowl, whisk together the Mustard Vinaigrette and Back Porch Mayo until they're thoroughly combined. Drizzle this dressing over the romaine halves.

Top the romaine with the tomatoes, chives, prosciutto, Garlic-Dill Pickled Onions and balsamic reduction (if using). Serve the wedge salads immediately.

dessert?
duh.

Desserts! As a family who enjoys celebrating special occasions, dessert was the course that was initially the most intimidating to make Paleo-friendly. How does one even make a Paleo cake, muffin or cookie? We had so much to learn! Once Makenna's gut was in a better place, we jumped right into the dessert adventure. There were still birthdays, holidays, bridal showers, weddings and other special occasions to celebrate—which means a delectable treat for most people. We've come so far in making sure all those occasions have the most decadent and oh-so-amazing Paleo-friendly treats as well.

In what is arguably the most loaded chapter in this book, you'll find some of our beloved family recipes. A few have culinary memories reaching back several generations, paying homage to loved ones no longer with us. We've re-created recipes like DeVona's Chocolate Pudding Cake (page 96), a luscious chocolate cake baked up in a warm chocolate pudding. Grant's Graham Cracker Cookies (page 99) is a very functional cookie born out of necessity, using what folks had on hand back in the early 1920s. Piparkakut Cookies (Finnish Gingersnaps; page 119) keep us in touch with our cherished Finnish roots. And then there are the Individual Fruit Pizzas (page 113), a recipe that allows everyone to use the toppings they want . . . less arguing, more eating and laughing!

devona's chocolate pudding cake

How this cake makes pudding while it bakes, we don't know. We're thrilled that it does, though. No bowls are required for this one—you mix it all up in the cake pan and let it do its magic while it bakes. This pudding cake is hands down the most-requested dessert when all of Michelle's siblings gather and enjoy a meal together. Adults love it, kids love it and—since it's easy to prep—the little ones can even help make it. DeVona's original recipe used a boxed cake mix and boxed pudding, so we built this version from the ground up. Read through this recipe a couple of times so that you'll know how to use the divided maple sugar and cocoa powder accordingly. One portion is for the cake, and the other part creates the pudding while it bakes. Make this cake and be amazed!

yield: 1 (8 x 8–inch [20 x 20–cm]) cake

¾ cup (100 g) cassava flour

1½ cups (282 g) maple sugar, divided

6 tbsp (30 g) unsweetened cocoa powder, divided

2 tsp (8 g) baking powder

¼ tsp plus ⅛ tsp fine sea salt, divided

1 large egg, at room temperature

½ cup (120 ml) full-fat coconut milk

2 tbsp (30 ml) avocado oil

1 tsp pure vanilla extract

1½ cups (360 ml) boiling water

Dairy-free ice cream or dairy-free whipped cream, for serving (optional)

Preheat the oven to 350°F (177°C).

In an ungreased 8 x 8–inch (20 x 20–cm) cake pan, stir together the cassava flour, ¾ cup (141 g) of the maple sugar, 2 tablespoons (10 g) of the cocoa powder, baking powder and ¼ teaspoon of the salt with a fork. Add the egg, coconut milk, avocado oil and vanilla. Mix the ingredients together until the batter is smooth and the egg is fully incorporated. The batter will be thick.

Spread the batter evenly in the cake pan. Sprinkle the remaining ¾ cup (141 g) of maple sugar, the remaining 4 tablespoons (20 g) of cocoa powder and the remaining ⅛ teaspoon of salt on top of the batter. Do *not* stir these ingredients into the batter.

Place the cake pan on a 13 x 18–inch (33 x 45–cm) baking sheet—in case of spillage—then pour the boiling water on top of the batter and again, do *not* stir the ingredients. Make sure all of the sugar-cocoa mixture is submerged by lightly tapping it down with a fork or butter knife—all of the dry mixture needs to be covered by the water.

Bake the cake for 35 to 40 minutes, or until a toothpick inserted into the center of the cake portion comes out clean. Don't push the toothpick in too far, or you'll end up in the pudding and not the cake. Remove the cake from the oven and let it rest for 10 to 15 minutes. The pudding will be on the bottom and very hot. Serve the pudding cake topped with the ice cream or whipped cream (if using).

grant's graham cracker cookies

This recipe is a throwback to Michelle's maternal grandfather (Makenna's great grandfather!), Grant. He was a child in the 1920s, and ingredients back then were often simple and could be hard to find. We make these cookies with our Honey Graham Crackers (page 86) and just a few other ingredients. The tasty chocolate frosting nestled between two graham crackers is simple and yet so special. Need an afternoon activity for the little ones? This recipe can be that activity. Need a sweet little something after lunch? Yep, you guessed it, here it is. These cookies are actually best the next day, as the frosting softens the graham crackers just enough that you can take a bite without the frosting squeezing out. Our family has been making these for several generations, and we're guessing that they will quickly become a favorite in your home too.

yield: 9 to 10 cookies

1 batch Honey Graham Crackers (page 86)

2½ cups (330 g) organic powdered sugar, plus additional if needed

1 tbsp (5 g) unsweetened cocoa powder

2 tbsp (30 ml) plain unsweetened almond milk, plus additional if needed

1 oz (28 g) dairy-free cream cheese (optional)

Bake the Honey Graham Crackers as directed on page 86, and let them cool completely before continuing with this recipe.

In a small bowl, combine the powdered sugar, cocoa powder, almond milk and cream cheese (if using). Use a hand mixer to beat the ingredients together until they're smooth. Add more milk or powdered sugar to reach your desired consistency. The frosting should be soft enough to spread but firm enough that it won't drip out from between the graham crackers.

Spread about 1 tablespoon (8 g) of the frosting on one Honey Graham Cracker, then place another cracker on top and press down to create a sandwich cookie. Repeat this process with the remaining frosting and Honey Graham Crackers.

For best results, let these cookies sit for at least 2 hours before serving. The frosting in the middle will soften up the cookies, so that they are easier to eat. They're even better after being left out overnight, and they can be stored at room temperature for up to 5 days.

mint-lanos

These cookies are insanely delicious! The melt-in-your-mouth cookie sandwiching the chocolate and mint filling is so irresistible. We named these Mint-lanos after asking our Instagram followers for help and this mash-up was a resounding winner. In our pre-Paleo days, we enjoyed them during every road trip, soccer game, volleyball match or drive-in movie we went to. Essentially, they're the perfect portable dessert. We are so thrilled to enjoy them once again, and we hope you will find that they are easier to make than you might think.

yield: 18 sandwich cookies or 36 individual cookies

¾ cup (100 g) cassava flour

½ tsp fine sea salt

½ cup (114 g) grass-fed butter, softened

⅔ cup (125 g) maple sugar

1 tsp pure vanilla extract

1 large egg, at room temperature

On a flat work surface, lay out two 13 x 18-inch (33 x 45-cm) pieces of parchment paper. Using a pencil or fine-tip permanent marker, trace ¾ x 2-inch (2 x 5-cm) ovals onto each piece of parchment paper, spacing the ovals about 1 inch (2.5 cm) apart. Alternatively, you can trace 2-inch (5-cm)-diameter circles onto the parchment paper, spacing the circles about 1 inch (2.5 cm) apart. Flip both pieces of parchment paper over and use them to line two 13 x 18-inch (33 x 45-cm) baking sheets.

In a small mixing bowl, whisk together the cassava flour and salt. Set the flour mixture aside.

In a medium bowl, combine the butter and maple sugar. Beat them well with a hand mixer at high speed for 2 to 3 minutes, until the mixture is light and fluffy. Add the vanilla and egg and mix again until the egg is completely combined with the fluffy mixture.

Add the flour mixture to the egg-butter mixture and, with the mixer running at low speed initially, beat the ingredients to combine them, increasing your speed once most of the cassava flour is incorporated.

Transfer the dough to a 1-gallon (3.8-L) ziplock bag. Squeeze the dough to one corner of the bag, and then carefully cut a ¾-inch (2-cm) opening from the corner with scissors. (Alternatively, you can use a piping bag fitted with a plain tip for this recipe.) Pipe the dough onto the prepared baking sheets, following the traced patterns. You should get approximately 36 individual cookies.

Chill the unbaked cookies in the refrigerator for 20 minutes. Meanwhile, preheat the oven to 325°F (163°C).

(continued)

mint-lanos (cont.)

4 oz (112 g) dairy-free dark
chocolate chips

¾ cup (90 g) organic powdered
sugar or maple powdered sugar

4 tsp (20 ml) water

2 drops food-grade peppermint
essential oil or ¼ tsp pure
peppermint extract

Once the unbaked cookies are done chilling, bake them for 12 to
14 minutes, or until the edges are just beginning to turn brown. Remove
the cookies from the oven and let them cool completely on the baking
sheets before transferring them to a cooling rack.

Prepare the filling for the cookies by placing the chocolate in a small
microwave-safe bowl and warming it in 20-second intervals until it is
melted, stirring the chocolate between each interval. Alternatively, you
can place the chocolate in a heatproof bowl and melt it over a double
boiler. In another small bowl, mix together the powdered sugar, water
and peppermint essential oil until the ingredients are smooth.

To assemble the sandwich cookies, use a butter knife to dab about
½ teaspoon of the chocolate on the flat side of half of the cookies.
Spread about ½ teaspoon of the peppermint glaze on the flat side of
the remaining half of the cookies. Let the chocolate and peppermint
glaze set up for 5 to 7 minutes, then sandwich opposing cookie halves
together. There should be just enough filling on each half to flatten
out and come to the edges of the sandwich cookie when you press the
halves together. Try a tester cookie initially, so you know for sure how
much chocolate and peppermint glaze to dab on each cookie.

Store these cookies at room temperature in an airtight container for up
to 4 days.

raspberry sherbet pie bars

Everyone always wants their piece of the pie. We've just made it a lot easier for you by turning our raspberry sherbet pie into bars! This pie is a favorite of ours in the summertime, when the raspberries are ripe. On many summer nights in Utah, this creamy frozen treat has provided a sweet relief to the heat. The conversion to bars seemed like a natural transition, as it's much easier to grab a small piece when you just can't take the warm temperatures anymore. We recommend having these on hand in the freezer all summer long.

yield: 16 bars

filling

12 oz (336 g) fresh raspberries plus 3 oz (84 g) fresh raspberries (optional), divided

1 cup (240 ml) pure maple syrup

¼ cup (60 ml) fresh lime juice

¾ cup (180 ml) full-fat coconut milk or nut milk of choice

1 tsp fine sea salt

1 tsp pure vanilla extract

1½ cups (360 ml) dairy-free vanilla yogurt

crust

½ cup (114 g) grass-fed butter, softened

⅓ cup (63 g) maple sugar

1 tsp pure vanilla extract

1 cup (133 g) cassava flour

¼ tsp fine sea salt

To make the filling, combine 12 ounces (336 g) of the raspberries, maple syrup and lime juice in a large saucepan over medium-low heat. Bring the mixture to a gentle simmer and cook it for about 10 minutes, stirring it occasionally. You want the raspberries to begin to break apart. Place a fine-mesh sieve over a large glass bowl and pour the hot liquid into it, so that you can strain out the raspberry seeds.

Once the raspberry liquid is strained, add the coconut milk, salt and vanilla. Place the mixture in the refrigerator for about 1 hour to cool slightly. Remove the mixture from the fridge and add the yogurt. Whisk the ingredients well to combine them, then cover the bowl and allow the mixture to chill in the fridge for a minimum of 4 hours, or overnight for the best results.

To make the crust, preheat the oven to 350°F (177°C). Prepare a 9 x 9–inch (23 x 23–cm) baking pan by lining it with parchment paper on the bottom and up the sides. Set the baking pan aside.

In a medium bowl, combine the butter, maple sugar and vanilla. Use a hand mixer to whip the ingredients together for 45 to 60 seconds, until they are combined and fluffy. Add the cassava flour and salt to the butter mixture and mix the ingredients again for 30 to 45 seconds, until the dough comes together. It will be crumbly, but don't worry.

(continued)

raspberry sherbet pie bars (cont.)

Press the dough evenly into the bottom of the prepared baking pan, then bake the crust for 13 to 15 minutes, or until it is just beginning to brown. Remove the crust from the oven and, while it is still warm, place a piece of parchment paper carefully on top of the crust and press down slightly on the crust's entire surface with a flat-bottomed glass. Then remove the top piece of parchment paper and allow the crust to cool completely in the pan.

To assemble the pie bars, freeze the raspberry mixture in your ice cream maker according to the manufacturer's instructions. If you are adding the optional remaining 3 ounces (84 g) of fresh raspberries, pour the frozen raspberry yogurt into a bowl and stir in the fresh raspberries to combine them with the yogurt base and break them apart. Pour the entire mixture into the prepared crust and place the pie in the freezer to firm up for at least 6 hours; for the best results, freeze the bars overnight.

To serve the pie bars, take the bars out of the freezer about 15 minutes ahead of time, so it's easier to slice. Slice the bars into 16 pieces and serve them. Store any leftovers in the freezer for up to 1 month.

anzac biscuits

When traveling around Australia and New Zealand, there's a specific kind of snack that seems to pop up at every petrol station: Anzac biscuits! *Anzac* stands for "Australian and New Zealand Army Corps." It is said that during World War I, these biscuits were sent by women's groups to soldiers abroad. The lack of eggs in these biscuits made for a perfect shelf-stable treat. New Zealand is one of our family's favorite travel destinations—this biscuit recipe brings back memories of driving from Queenstown to Milford Sound, snacking away as the hills filled with sheep go by.

yield: 16 cookies

¾ cup (100 g) cassava flour
1 cup (99 g) tiger nut flakes
¾ cup (141 g) maple sugar
¾ cup (64 g) unsweetened desiccated coconut (see Note)
⅛ tsp fine sea salt
½ cup (114 g) grass-fed butter
2 tbsp (30 ml) pure maple syrup
1 tsp baking soda
2 tbsp (30 ml) boiling water

Note: It's important to use the fine-textured desiccated coconut and not the coarser shredded coconut. Otherwise, the cookies will flatten out too much.

Preheat the oven to 350°F (177°C). Line two 13 x 18–inch (33 x 45–cm) baking sheets with parchment paper or silicone baking mats.

In a medium bowl, mix together the cassava flour, tiger nut flakes, maple sugar, coconut and salt. Set the flour mixture aside.

In a small saucepan over medium heat, combine the butter and maple syrup. Warm the mixture, stirring it occasionally, until the butter has melted and the mixture is bubbly.

While the butter and maple syrup are warming, combine the baking soda and boiling water in a medium bowl and whisk them vigorously. The mixture should foam slightly. Once the butter and maple syrup are bubbling, add the baking soda–water mixture in a slow stream, whisking the butter-maple mixture constantly. The mixture should foam up once again.

Add the butter-maple mixture to the flour mixture. Use a hand mixer to combine the two mixtures until there are no clumps.

Firmly pack the biscuit dough into a 1½-tablespoon (23-g) cookie scoop. Then gently form the dough into a ball. Once the ball is formed, place it on one of the prepared baking sheets. Repeat this process with the remaining dough, spacing each biscuit about 2 inches (5 cm) apart.

Bake the biscuits for 15 minutes, until they are mostly flattened but still have an edge and they are golden.

Let the biscuits cool until they are firm enough to handle. Store the biscuits in an airtight container at room temperature for up to 1 week, or freeze them for up to 3 months.

crunchy cookie ice cream

When you have extra cookies that you think might go bad before you can eat all of them, this dessert is the answer. This Paleo-friendly ice cream is a versatile recipe in that you can pretty much use whatever cookies you have, although we have included some suggestions in the ingredient list that we love and think you'll love too! Sometimes simple is best, and a vanilla ice cream base with cookie chunks has never failed us in the taste department. We've been known to have a container of this ice cream in the freezer at all times, as it's a delightfully creamy treat that hits all the right spots.

yield: 4 servings

2 (14-oz [420-ml]) cans full-fat coconut milk or 3½ cups (840 ml) nut milk of choice, divided

½ cup (120 ml) pure maple syrup or raw honey, plus additional if needed

¼ tsp fine sea salt

1 vanilla bean, seeds scraped out, or ⅛ tsp vanilla powder

2 tbsp (16 g) cassava flour

1½ tsp (8 ml) pure vanilla extract

1 cup (240 g) crumbled Anzac Biscuits (page 106), Piparkakut Cookies (Finnish Gingersnaps; page 119) or Mint-lanos (page 100), plus additional as needed (optional)

In a large, heavy-bottomed saucepan over medium heat, combine 3 cups (720 ml) of the coconut milk, maple syrup, salt and vanilla bean seeds. Bring the mixture to a simmer, stirring it occasionally.

Meanwhile, mix together the remaining ½ cup (120 ml) of coconut milk with the cassava flour in a small bowl to make a slurry. Set the slurry aside.

Once the vanilla milk is warm, whisk in the slurry until the two are well combined and the mixture thickens a bit. Remove the mixture from the heat and taste it, adding additional sweetener if desired. Stir in the vanilla. Pour the ice cream mixture into a medium container. Refrigerate the mixture for a minimum of 4 hours, or overnight for the best results.

Using an ice cream maker, make the ice cream according to the manufacturer's directions. Transfer the ice cream to a large bowl and stir in the crushed cookies. Transfer the ice cream to a freezer-safe container and place it in the freezer to firm up. Serve the ice cream with additional cookies (if using).

rustic herbed cherry galette

Developing a Paleo pie crust recipe was a labor of love several years ago after cassava flour rolled onto the scene. Pies have always been enjoyed year-round by our family, and we were thrilled to perfect this crust recipe. So if you're looking to enjoy the flavors of a classic cherry pie without the extra effort often required for an actual pie, this galette is an awesome option. We paired tart cherries with fresh thyme for a subtle savory element. It's superb and is a flavor combo that will surprise your taste buds. The best thing is that we used frozen cherries, so if you have a bag hanging out in the freezer, this baked treat is ready in no time.

yield: 6 to 8 servings

1 uncooked Paleo Pie Crust (page 131)

4 cups (616 g) frozen tart cherries, slightly thawed

¼ cup (47 g) maple sugar, plus additional for dusting (optional)

3 tbsp (24 g) cassava flour

½ tsp finely chopped fresh thyme

¼ tsp fine sea salt

Zest and juice from 1 (2-oz [56-g]) lime

1 large egg

Whipped coconut cream or dairy-free vanilla ice cream (optional)

Preheat the oven to 415°F (213°C). Prepare the Paleo Pie Crust as directed on page 131, rolling it out to approximately 13 to 14 inches (33 to 36 cm) in diameter. Leave it on the parchment paper and slide it onto a 13 x 18–inch (33 x 45–cm) baking sheet.

In a large bowl, combine the cherries, maple sugar, cassava flour, thyme, salt, lime zest and lime juice. Using a rubber spatula, stir the ingredients to coat the cherries. Mash a few cherries slightly with the back of the spatula.

Mound the filling into the center of the pie crust, leaving an approximately 2½-inch (6-cm) border of crust around the filling that you'll fold over it.

Using the parchment paper, lift up and carefully fold the dough over the filling by about 2 inches (5 cm), working your way around the circle, pleating dough if necessary, until the dough is all folded up over the filling but the cherries in the center are still exposed.

Crack the egg into a small cup and mix it well. Using a pastry brush, coat the dough with the egg wash and dust it with the additional maple sugar (if using).

Bake the galette for 40 to 45 minutes, or until the filling is bubbly in the middle and the crust is golden brown.

Remove the galette from the oven and let it cool until the filling is set. Slice the galette and serve it as is, or serve it with the whipped coconut cream or your favorite dairy-free vanilla ice cream (if using).

individual fruit pizzas

For many years, a fruit pizza was a guaranteed staple at almost every celebratory event for our family. Birthday party? Yep. Graduations? For sure. Weddings, even? Absolutely. This is a delightfully bright dessert because it's covered in the most beautiful fresh fruits. The special thing about this recipe is that the pizzas are individual—the customization is sure to make these a hit at your next celebratory gathering!

yield: 12 (4½-inch [11-cm]) round cookies and 2½ cups (280 g) frosting

cookies

½ cup (120 ml) dairy-free sour cream

½ tsp baking soda

2 cups (266 g) cassava flour, plus additional as needed

1 cup (188 g) maple sugar

1 tsp baking powder

¼ tsp fine sea salt

½ cup (96 g) organic vegetable shortening

2 large eggs, at room temperature

1 tsp pure vanilla extract

½ tsp apple cider vinegar

To make the cookies, preheat the oven to 400°F (204°C). Prepare two 13 x 18-inch (33 x 45-cm) baking sheets by lining them with parchment paper or silicone baking mats.

In a small bowl that can hold at least 1 cup (240 ml), combine the sour cream and baking soda, stirring them well. This mixture will "bloom," so that's why it is important to make sure your bowl can hold at least 1 cup (240 ml). Set the bowl aside.

In a medium bowl, whisk together the cassava flour, maple sugar, baking powder and salt. Set the flour mixture aside.

In another medium bowl, combine the shortening, eggs, vanilla and apple cider vinegar. Using a hand mixer, whip the ingredients for 45 to 60 seconds, until they are fluffy. Add the flour mixture to the shortening mixture, initially mixing slowly to avoid a puff of flour and increasing the mixer's speed until the two mixtures are incorporated. The mixture will be crumbly. Add the sour cream mixture and continue mixing for 30 to 45 seconds, until the dough comes together.

Divide the dough in half. Leave one half in the bowl, covered, while you roll out the other half. Lay down a 13 x 18-inch (33 x 45-cm) piece of parchment paper and lightly dust it with the additional cassava flour. Place the first half of the dough in the center of the parchment paper, dusting it with more cassava flour. Grab an additional 13 x 18-inch (33 x 45-cm) piece of parchment paper, and place it on top of the dough.

(continued)

individual fruit pizzas (cont.)

frosting

8 oz (224 g) dairy-free cream cheese

1 cup (120 g) organic powdered sugar

½ tsp pure vanilla extract

suggested toppings

Kiwi

Strawberries

Mango

Raspberries

Blueberries

Dragon fruit

Roll out the dough between the pieces of parchment paper until it is approximately ¼ inch (6 mm) thick, lightly dusting the dough and parchment paper with the cassava flour as needed. Cut out the cookies as desired—we use a 4½-inch (11-cm) round cookie cutter. Place the cookies on the prepared baking sheets, spacing the cookies 1 inch (2.5 cm) apart. Reroll the dough scraps until the dough is completely used. Repeat these steps with the other half of the dough.

Bake the cookies for 8 to 10 minutes, or until the edges just begin to turn brown. Remove the cookies from the oven and let them cool completely before moving.

While the cookies cool, make the frosting. In a small bowl, use a hand mixer to combine the cream cheese, powdered sugar and vanilla for approximately 60 seconds, until the frosting is fluffy. If you're enjoying the fruit pizzas right away, spread each cookie with the desired amount of frosting and top each individual pizza with some of our suggested toppings, or whatever your favorites are. If you like a lot of frosting on each pizza, you may want to make a double batch of frosting. If you're not enjoying the fruit pizzas right away, wait to frost the cookies until right before you serve them.

The cookies can be made ahead of time. Store them in a freezer-safe container, separated by parchment paper, in the freezer for up to 2 months. The frosting can be made ahead of time but is best used within 3 to 4 days.

raspberry lemonade jell-o

Our raspberry lemonade Jello-O is, in fact, a remake of our beloved Patsy's lemon Jell-O. All you have to do is mention the name, and everyone in our family will gasp, hoping it will be on the dinner table with our Lemon Chicken, which is a hit on our blog. Our Patsy was well known for her famous molded salads—she was a regular gelatin magician. Remaking her recipe with natural ingredients required some work, since she and most everyone else made these offerings with boxed gelatin. We did it, though. This Jell-O is exactly what our taste buds remember. We serve this as a side dish with a meal, but you can also easily serve it as dessert.

yield: 6 cups (1.6 kg) molded Jell-O

2½ tbsp (15 g) unflavored powdered gelatin

3 cups (720 ml) cold water, divided

6 oz (168 g) fresh raspberries

½ cup (120 ml) pure maple syrup

¾ cup (180 ml) raw honey

¾ cup (180 ml) fresh lemon juice

1 tsp lemon zest

8 drops food-grade lemon essential oil

¼ tsp fine sea salt

2 cups (480 ml) dairy-free whipped cream, plus additional for topping (optional)

Fruits of choice, for serving

In a small bowl, combine the gelatin and 1 cup (240 ml) of the cold water. Set this mixture aside and allow the gelatin to soften for about 5 minutes.

While the gelatin softens, combine 1 cup (240 ml) of the cold water, raspberries and maple syrup in a saucepan. Bring this mixture to a boil over high heat, then reduce the heat to medium-low and allow the mixture to simmer for 5 to 7 minutes, stirring it occasionally, until the raspberries break apart.

Place a strainer over an 8-cup (1.9-L) glass bowl and pour the raspberry mixture through it, straining out the seeds. Add the softened gelatin to this raspberry mixture and whisk the two to dissolve the gelatin and fully combine the ingredients. Discard the strained raspberry seeds.

Add the remaining 1 cup (240 ml) of cold water, honey, lemon juice, lemon zest, lemon essential oil and salt to the warm gelatin mixture. Whisk the ingredients together to fully combine everything. Set the gelatin in the fridge for 50 to 60 minutes to allow it to set up slightly. It should just barely be starting to thicken up.

Remove the gelatin from the fridge, add the whipped cream and use a hand mixer to combine it fully with the gelatin. Pour the gelatin into a 6-cup (1.4-L) mold. Refrigerate the gelatin overnight for the best results.

To serve the Jell-O, select a rimmed plate or a platter that will accommodate the width of the mold you used.

(continued)

raspberry lemonade jell-o (cont.)

Pull the Jell-O slightly from the sides of the mold—if the Jell-O seems stuck, you can dunk the bottom of the mold in a dish of warm water for about 10 seconds to release it. Invert the serving plate on top of the mold, then carefully flip the two over and give them a little jiggle. The Jell-O should drop down onto the serving plate from the mold; if not, give it another little jiggle until it releases.

Arrange the fruit as desired either around the molded Jell-O or inside the center cavity. Add the additional whipped cream (if using) either on top of the Jell-O or inside the center cavity. Serve this Jell-O right away and store any leftovers in the fridge in an airtight container for up to 5 days.

piparkakut cookies (finnish gingersnaps)

Our dearest Patsy hailed from Finland; her parents were immigrants who came to the United States many years ago. It's important to honor those roots, as we all have to remember our humble beginnings. Similar to a gingersnap, this addicting cookie is ideal for the holiday season.

yield: 36 (3½-inch [9-cm]-diameter) cookies

1¾ cups (233 g) cassava flour, plus additional as needed

1½ tsp (7 g) baking soda

½ tsp fine sea salt

6 tbsp (120 g) blackstrap molasses

½ cup (94 g) maple sugar

½ cup (114 g) grass-fed butter

1 tsp ground cinnamon

1 tsp ground ginger

1 tsp ground cloves

1 large egg, beaten and at room temperature

1 cup (240 ml) ice water

Organic powdered sugar, as needed (optional)

In a small bowl, sift together the cassava flour, baking soda and salt. Set the flour mixture aside. In a large saucepan over medium heat, whisk together the molasses, maple sugar, butter, cinnamon, ginger and cloves. Bring the mixture to a boil, then remove it from the heat. Allow the molasses mixture to cool for about 20 minutes, then add the egg. Beat the ingredients together with a hand mixer for 60 to 90 seconds, until the mixture is fluffy and lighter in color.

Add the flour mixture to the molasses-egg mixture and beat the two to combine them. Let the dough sit for about 5 minutes, and don't be alarmed: The dough will be very loose at this point. Lay a large piece of plastic wrap on a work surface, and then transfer the dough to the center of the plastic wrap and wrap the dough in the plastic. Refrigerate the dough overnight.

The next day, preheat the oven to 390°F (199°C). Prepare two 13 x 18-inch (33 x 45-cm) baking sheets by lining them with parchment paper. Cut the dough in half and return one half to the fridge while you work with the first half.

Lay one 13 x 18-inch (33 x 45-cm) piece of parchment paper on a work surface and generously dust with additional cassava flour. Place the dough in the center of the parchment paper. Dust it with a little more cassava flour and lay an additional piece of parchment paper of the same size on top. Roll out the dough as thinly as possible between the two pieces of parchment paper. Cut out the cookies in your desired shape, and place them about 1 inch (2.5 cm) apart on the prepared baking sheets. Reroll the scraps and cut out additional cookies until the dough is gone. Then repeat these steps with the second half of the dough.

Before baking the cookies, carefully brush each one with the ice water. Bake the cookies for 6 to 8 minutes, or until they are slightly puffy and brown. Remove the cookies from the oven and transfer them to a cooling rack. These little gems will crisp up as they cool. Dust them with the powdered sugar (if using) and serve them. They can be stored at room temperature for up to 1 week.

haupia tropical fruit tart

It's probably obvious at this point in the book that we have a deep love for island life and all things tropical. Haupia is traditionally a coconut pudding that you may have enjoyed if you've visited the islands of Hawaii. Since coconut milk is naturally dairy-free, this delicious and Paleo-friendly twist on the island treat was a must. The scrumptious, subtly sweet filling lives in a baked crust of shredded coconut and macadamia nuts. We've topped ours with cubed mango, kiwi and dragon fruit, then we've garnished it all with passion fruit. A truly unique flavor experience awaits you, and we're confident you will feel warm tropical breezes wafting over your cheeks with every bite.

yield: 4 servings

crust

1¼ cups (116 g) unsweetened desiccated coconut

¼ cup (31 g) raw macadamia nuts, finely chopped

1 tbsp (8 g) cassava flour

3 tbsp (45 ml) melted coconut oil

2 tbsp (30 ml) pure maple syrup

1 tsp pure vanilla extract

⅛ tsp fine sea salt

filling

¼ cup (60 ml) cold water

½ tbsp (3 g) unflavored powdered gelatin

¾ cup (180 ml) full-fat coconut milk

½ cup (120 ml) plain unsweetened almond milk

¼ cup (47 g) maple sugar

⅛ tsp fine sea salt

To make the crust, preheat the oven to 350°F (177°C). Line the bottom of a 5 x 14–inch (13 x 35–cm) rectangular tart pan or an 8-inch (20-cm) round tart pan with parchment paper. If you do not have a tart pan, line a 9 x 9–inch (23 x 23–cm) baking pan with parchment paper.

In a medium bowl, use a fork to mix together the coconut, macadamia nuts and cassava flour. Add the coconut oil, maple syrup, vanilla and salt. Mix the ingredients together with a small spoon to thoroughly blend the wet and dry ingredients.

Press the crust mixture evenly into the bottom and up the sides of the prepared tart pan. Alternatively, if you are using a square baking pan, press the crust mixture into the bottom of the pan.

Bake the crust for 10 to 12 minutes, or until the edges just begin to turn brown. Remove the crust from the oven and let the crust cool completely.

To make the filling, pour the cold water into a small bowl and sprinkle the gelatin over the top of the water. Allow the gelatin to soften for about 5 minutes.

In a small saucepan over medium-low heat, combine the coconut milk, almond milk, maple sugar and salt. Warm the mixture for 5 to 6 minutes, stirring it occasionally, until it is just simmering and the sugar has melted.

(continued)

haupia tropical fruit tart (cont.)

suggested toppings

Mango
Kiwi
Dragon fruit
Passion fruit

Remove the milk mixture from the heat and add the softened gelatin, whisking the two to combine them. Do not pour the filling into the tart crust yet, since it's hot and thin; it will seep right into the crust. Instead, pour the mixture into a medium bowl and place it in the refrigerator for 45 to 60 minutes to allow the filling to set slightly. It should be thick enough to coat your finger but not firm enough that it feels like you can push on it and leave an indentation. Keep an eye on it, as you don't want it to set up too much; otherwise, it won't pour easily into the tart crust.

Once the filling is slightly set, pour it into the prepared tart crust and place the tart in the refrigerator to chill for 60 to 90 minutes, until the center no longer jiggles when the tart is gently shaken.

When you are ready to serve the tart, pop it out of the pan and place it on a serving platter. Top the tart with the mango, kiwi, dragon fruit and passion fruit, then slice and serve it.

milk chocolate cream pie

We can't think of a tastier filling to pour into our beloved Paleo Pie Crust (page 131) than this dreamy chocolate goodness. If you're looking for a chocolate fix, look no further—this is it! The filling is a dairy-free, silky delight with a very mellow chocolate flavor, so two pieces might be in order. If you prefer a darker chocolate flavor, feel free to increase the cocoa powder by 1 tablespoon (5 g), then dive into the rich and deep side of dark chocolate. Either way, cut into this delicious pie and enjoy every single bite.

yield: 1 (9-inch [23-cm]) pie

6 large egg yolks, at room temperature

½ cup (94 g) maple sugar

3 tbsp (24 g) tapioca starch

¼ cup (22 g) unsweetened cocoa powder

½ tsp fine sea salt

1½ cups (360 ml) plain unsweetened almond milk

3 tbsp (42 g) grass-fed butter or ghee

2 tsp (10 ml) pure vanilla extract

1½ cups (360 ml) dairy-free whipped cream, divided

1 baked Paleo Pie Crust (page 131)

Shaved dairy-free chocolate, for garnishing (optional)

Prepare a large heatproof bowl with a fine-mesh sieve on top of it. Set the bowl aside.

In a medium bowl, combine the egg yolks and maple sugar. Whip the ingredients with a hand mixer for 1 to 2 minutes, until they are well combined and a little lighter in color. Add the tapioca starch, cocoa powder and salt and mix them well into the egg-sugar mixture.

Pour in the almond milk and mix the ingredients again to fully combine them. Pour this mixture into a large, heavy-bottomed saucepan. Cook the mixture over medium heat for 5 to 7 minutes, stirring it constantly, until it has thickened. Remove the custard from the heat and whisk in the butter and vanilla.

Pour the custard through the fine-mesh sieve into the bowl, using the back of a spoon to push it through. The custard will be thick, but this process will remove any lumps, making for a very creamy texture.

Place the custard in the refrigerator to cool for 45 to 60 minutes. When the custard is cool, add 1 cup (240 ml) of the whipped cream and fold it into the custard with a rubber spatula to combine the two. Pour the pie filling into the prepared Paleo Pie Crust. Place the pie in the refrigerator for at least 4 hours, or up to overnight for the best results, to allow the filling to set up.

When you are ready to serve the pie, place the remaining ½ cup (120 ml) of the whipped cream in the center of the pie and sprinkle the shaved chocolate on top (if using).

*See photo on page 94.

mango sweet rice

If you tolerate basmati rice on occasion like we do, you are going to enjoy this dessert. Traditionally you may see this called mango sticky rice, Thai sweet rice and mango or sticky rice with mango—there are so many variations. This dessert is another recipe that gives us such warm fuzzies! While it's one we usually don't make at home, we would *always* enjoy it at our favorite Thai restaurant when we were visiting family in St. George, Utah. After a tasty family meal there, we would make sure we had several orders of mango sticky rice to share. Everyone grabbed a spoon to enjoy their portion. The rice and sauce are warm and slightly sweet, and—when they are paired with fresh mango—eating this dish is one of those "oh my" moments you're not likely to forget. We hope you enjoy our take on this beloved dessert filled with family memories of sitting around a table and eating together.

yield: 5 (½-cup [50-g]) servings

rice

1 cup (200 g) basmati rice

2 cups (480 ml) water

¾ cup (180 ml) full-fat coconut milk

½ cup (94 g) maple sugar

¼ tsp fine sea salt

sauce

1 cup (240 ml) full-fat coconut milk

2 tbsp (24 g) maple sugar

2 tbsp (16 g) tapioca starch

½ tsp fine sea salt

toppings

2 large Ataulfo mangoes, cut into ¼" (6-mm)-thick slices

1 tbsp (9 g) sesame seeds (optional)

To make the rice, combine the rice and water in a large saucepan. Bring the water to a boil over medium-high heat, then cover the saucepan and reduce the heat to low. Simmer the rice for 15 to 20 minutes, or until it is fluffy.

While the rice cooks, prepare the soaking liquid for the rice by combining the coconut milk, maple sugar and salt in a small saucepan. Bring the mixture to a boil over medium-low heat, stirring it occasionally, until the sugar is dissolved. Pour the hot liquid over the cooked rice in the large saucepan and stir it to combine. Let this cool, covered, for 1 hour.

Once the rice has cooled, make the sauce. In a medium saucepan, whisk together the coconut milk, maple sugar, tapioca starch and salt. Warm the mixture over medium-low heat for 3 to 5 minutes, until the maple sugar is dissolved, the mixture has thickened a bit and it is bubbly.

To serve, transfer ½ cup (50 g) of the sweet rice to a serving plate and shape it as desired. Drizzle 2 tablespoons (30 ml) of the warm topping sauce over the rice, arrange the mango slices on top of the rice and garnish it with the sesame seeds (if using). Serve the sweet rice immediately.

everyday basics

In the cooking world, there are always some recipes that tie dishes together and take them over the top. They are generally kitchen staples and are quite versatile, allowing you to use them in a variety of recipes. The biggest problem is that most of these traditional recipes use highly processed oils, sugars, gluten and dairy, which do not get along with our bellies. We're happy to report that we've revamped these classic recipes in a way that leaves our guts feeling happy and our taste buds satisfied!

Dig a little deeper into this chapter's contents and you'll find the building blocks for tasty kitchen adventures. Our Hamburger Buns (page 128) and Paleo Pie Crust (page 131) open the door for many savory and sweet creations. Our Back Porch Mayo (page 134), which we make weekly, is incredibly versatile. And we're confident you'll find yourself adding our Garlic-Dill Pickled Onions (page 137) to so many dishes. The offerings in this chapter pair well with several of the recipes included in this book, but we encourage you to be creative and try them on other recipes as well. You'll be surprised what tasty endeavors await you.

hamburger buns

This bun recipe was years in the making, and all our attempts really paid off. These buns have a great texture and lots of airy bubbles—they are an excellent vessel for Patsy's Sloppy Joes (page 58) or your next burger. Ultimately, they are a riff on our Patsy's sweet roll recipe from our blog, in which she uses mashed potatoes to create a fantastic texture. Red bliss potatoes seem to lend the best texture, and these buns are even better if you use day-old mashed potatoes prepared like we do in our Cottage Pie (page 65). Working with yeast may seem intimidating, but you can do it! Read through the recipe a couple of times before you start and you'll be on your way.

yield: 6 hamburger buns

1 tsp coconut oil

½ cup (120 ml) 110°F (43°C) water

2 tbsp (30 ml) raw honey

4 tsp (16 g) quick-rise yeast

⅓ cup (80 ml) avocado oil or ⅓ cup (77 g) softened grass-fed butter

4 large eggs, at room temperature, divided

½ cup (125 g) mashed potatoes (page 65), at room temperature

1 tbsp (15 ml) apple cider vinegar

1½ tsp (9 g) fine sea salt

1¾ cups (233 g) cassava flour, divided, plus additional as needed

Sesame seeds, for topping (optional)

Preheat the oven to 400°F (204°C). Line a 13 x 18–inch (33 x 45–cm) baking sheet with parchment paper.

Now make foil rings to shape the buns by laying out six sheets of aluminum foil that are 15 to 17 inches (38 to 43 cm) long and 12 inches (30 cm) wide. Working with one sheet at a time, fold the sheet in half starting with the long edge, then fold it in half again and then fold it in half one more time. You're essentially making it one-eighth of the original size, so that you end up with a strip that is 15 x 1½ inches (38 x 3 cm). Alternatively, to shape the foil rings, you can use the bottom of a ramekin as a guide to get the diameter you want: Simply wrap the foil strip around the ramekin's base and fold over the edge to secure it. Head to our blog and our dedicated cookbook page for additional help and videos regarding this process. Coat the inside of each ring with the coconut oil. Set the rings aside.

In a glass 2-cup (480-ml) measuring cup, combine the water, honey and yeast. Whisk the ingredients together well and allow the yeast to bloom, or become frothy, which can take anywhere from 5 to 10 minutes. Using a glass measuring cup here will more easily allow you to see the yeast blooming and know when it's ready.

While the yeast blooms, combine the avocado oil, 3 of the eggs, mashed potatoes, apple cider vinegar and salt in a medium bowl. Using a hand mixer, beat the ingredients together until they are well combined.

(continued)

hamburger buns (cont.)

Place 1½ cups (200 g) of the cassava flour in a large bowl. Once the yeast has fully bloomed, pour that mixture and the oil-egg mixture into the flour. Beat the ingredients at slow speed until everything is combined, then beat them at medium-high speed for about 1 minute to fully combine them. Let the batter rest for 5 minutes. Check the consistency by touching the batter; if it sticks to your fingers, add 2 tablespoons (16 g) of the remaining ¼ cup (33 g) of cassava flour and mix the batter again. Let the batter rest for another 5 minutes. You should end up with approximately 3 cups (720 ml) of batter.

Sprinkle the remaining cassava flour on a clean work surface. Dust a spatula with additional cassava flour. Transfer ½ cup (120 ml) of the batter to the prepared work surface and dust the batter with a little additional cassava flour. Using the prepared spatula, lift the batter to your hands and shape it by gently rolling it back and forth until you have a smooth ball. Place the ball on the prepared baking sheet. Repeat this process with the remaining batter.

Gently flatten and shape each mound of batter with your fingers to get a slight dome. Whisk the remaining egg in a small cup and brush the top of each batter mound with the egg wash. Sprinkle each mound's top with the sesame seeds (if using), then place a foil ring around it.

Cover the buns with a kitchen towel and place the baking sheet in a warm area of your kitchen. Let the buns rise for 10 to 12 minutes. You don't want them to rise too much, or they'll begin cracking before they bake.

Place the baking sheet in the oven and immediately reduce the oven's temperature to 385°F (196°C). Bake the buns for 35 to 40 minutes, or until the tops are golden brown.

Remove the baking sheet from the oven, allow the buns to cool for 5 minutes, then remove the foil rings from them. If any of the rings are stuck, use a thin knife to loosen the foil rings away from the buns.

These buns are best served the day you make them, but they can be stored in the fridge and enjoyed the next day as well. We recommend letting them cool completely before slicing and toasting them.

paleo pie crust

This Paleo pie crust was a labor of love inspired by our momma DeVona and her pie-making skills, which she relied on heavily during the holidays. Learning how to make pie crust at a very young age was a rite of passage for our family, and we've made many over the years. When cassava flour hit the market in early 2015, our Paleo pie crust dreams became a reality, as did our hopes of once again enjoying pie during the holidays. Using cassava flour made it possible to tweak DeVona's recipe and use the technique she learned in junior high school in the 1950s. This recipe has been a blog favorite since it made its debut during the 2015 holidays and has been made by many new friends and followers. Knowing that so many are able to enjoy authentic pie crust again is truly heartwarming, and we're sure DeVona is pleased.

yield: 1 (9-inch [23-cm]) pie crust

1 cup (133 g) cassava flour, plus additional as needed

2 tbsp (16 g) arrowroot flour

¼ tsp fine sea salt

½ cup (96 g) organic vegetable shortening

1 large egg, beaten

¼ cup (60 ml) room-temperature water

Additional beaten egg (optional)

In a medium bowl, use a fork to combine the cassava flour, arrowroot flour and salt.

Add the shortening to the flour mixture and cut it into the ingredients with a pastry blender or a fork until it is incorporated and the mixture resembles coarse crumbs. Next, add the egg and stir the ingredients until they are combined. Add the water, mixing it into the flour mixture completely. Roll the dough around the bowl with your hands to clean the sides until the dough comes together in a smooth ball.

Lay a 13 x 18–inch (33 x 45–cm) piece of parchment paper on a work surface, and dust the parchment paper with a bit of additional cassava flour. Place the dough in the center of the parchment paper, then flatten it slightly into a disk and dust it with a little more cassava flour. Place another sheet of parchment paper on top of the dough and roll the dough into a large circle that is approximately ¼ inch (6 mm) thick. If you're going to be making our Rustic Herbed Cherry Galette, you can stop at this step and proceed with the filling as directed on page 110. For a traditional pie that's baked or filled, please see the remaining steps.

(continued)

paleo pie crust (cont.)

Pull the top piece of parchment paper back, dust the dough with a little flour, then lay it back down. Flip the entire crust over. Remove the top parchment paper and lay an ungreased 9-inch (23-cm) pie plate upside down in the center of the crust. Carefully flip the crust and pie plate over simultaneously and let the dough fall into the pie plate. Remove the parchment paper and pinch together any tears in the crust. Trim the dough on the sides of the pie plate. Reroll the leftover dough and use it for your desired finished pie edge.

To prebake the crust, preheat the oven to 400°F (204°C). Poke a few holes in the bottom and sides of the crust with a fork, allowing the steam to release during baking. If you are using an egg wash, bake the crust for 10 minutes, then remove it from the oven and brush the edges with the additional beaten egg. Bake the crust for 15 to 20 more minutes, or until it is golden brown. Cover the crust's edges with a pie crust shield if it begins to get too dark. If you choose not to use egg wash, bake the crust for 25 to 30 minutes, or until it is golden.

To make a filled crust, add your desired pie filling to the raw crust and bake the pie as directed in the recipe, covering the crust's edges if necessary.

For an instructional video on decorative edges on our pie crust and other tips, feel free to visit our website.

back porch mayo

Making our own mayonnaise was one of the first things we wanted to try early in our Paleo journey, when Makenna's health demanded that we make changes to her diet. Traditional mayo uses highly processed oils that are typically very inflammatory. When we made our first batch, we were so thrilled to see these simple ingredients come together and know that we could in fact make our own successfully. Early on we used olive oil and found that, depending on the brand, it can make a very strongly flavored mayonnaise. Since then, we've moved to using avocado oil, since it's mild in flavor. We like the addition of vinegar and salt in our variation along with the mustard—we think this combo makes the mayo's flavor more vibrant while still keeping it mild.

yield: 1¼ cups (300 ml)

1 large egg, at room temperature

1 tbsp (15 ml) Dijon mustard, at room temperature

1 tbsp (15 ml) red wine vinegar

1 tsp fresh lemon juice

¼ tsp fine sea salt

1 cup (240 ml) avocado oil

In a large Mason jar or a tall widemouthed jar, combine the egg, mustard, red wine vinegar, lemon juice, salt and avocado oil. Position the blade of an immersion blender right over the egg and begin blending, leaving the blade near the bottom of the jar for 2 to 3 seconds. Then slowly move the blender up and down until the egg and oil are completely emulsified. Alternatively, you can use a small food processor to make this mayo. In the food processor, combine the egg, mustard, red wine vinegar, lemon juice and salt. Process the ingredients, then, with the food processor running, add the oil in a slow stream until everything is emulsified.

Store the mayo in a lidded jar in the refrigerator for about 10 days.

garlic-dill pickled onions

We aren't sure about you, but we've never met a dish with pickled onions that we haven't liked: tacos, avocado toast, egg salad, tuna salad, green salad, pizza, sandwiches . . . the list goes on. These adorably pink and crunchy onions add the perfect zing to virtually any meal you're making. Not to mention that they're incredibly pretty and photogenic. We've been known to have a jar of pickled onions on hand in the fridge at all times because they're that good. We think that once you try them, you'll be hooked as well!

yield: 1 (20-ounce [560-g]) jar of onions

¾ cup (180 ml) filtered water

¾ cup (180 ml) apple cider vinegar

1½ tsp (8 ml) pure maple syrup

2 tsp (12 g) fine sea salt

1 medium red onion, very thinly sliced

1 tbsp (3 g) minced fresh dill or 1½ tsp (1 g) dried dill

3 to 4 cloves garlic, peeled and crushed

In a small saucepan over medium heat, combine the water, apple cider vinegar, maple syrup and salt. Bring the mixture to a simmer, stirring it occasionally, until the salt has dissolved—this will take 4 to 5 minutes.

Meanwhile, place the onion, dill and garlic in a 20-ounce (560-g) heatproof glass jar, tucking the dill and garlic around the onion as you place all the ingredients in the jar.

Once the water-vinegar mixture is simmering, carefully pour it into the jar over the onion. The glass jar will be very hot at this point, so please use caution.

Let the onions rest and cool for 30 minutes, then seal the jar with its lid. Place the jar in the refrigerator. Let the pickled onions cool in the refrigerator for a minimum of 1 hour before enjoying them. These get better with age, so they'll be even tastier the next day!

toasted pine nut arugula pesto

Pesto is the go-to for leftover greens that every kitchen needs. Do you have some arugula remaining from a recipe that you aren't quite sure what to do with? We highly recommend whipping up this pesto. The typically pepper-forward arugula gets tamed by the addition of toasted pine nuts and garlic. We have used this pesto for years on pizzas, pasta, sandwiches—you name it. It's a versatile sauce that we won't stop making any time soon!

yield: 1 cup (240 ml)

½ cup (68 g) pine nuts

2 tightly packed cups (40 g) arugula

2 to 3 cloves garlic, roughly chopped

2 tbsp (30 ml) red wine vinegar

1 tsp fine sea salt, plus additional if needed

¼ tsp black pepper, plus additional if needed

Juice of ½ large lemon, plus additional if needed

3 tbsp (45 ml) avocado oil

In a small, dry cast-iron skillet over low heat, toast the pine nuts for 5 to 7 minutes, stirring the nuts occasionally, until they are golden. Transfer them from the skillet to a small plate and let them cool completely.

Place the toasted pine nuts, arugula, garlic, red wine vinegar, salt, black pepper and lemon juice in the bowl of a small food processor. Pulse the ingredients to begin pulverizing them, using a small spatula to clean the sides of the bowl as needed.

With the food processor running, slowly add the avocado oil until everything is fully combined. Taste the pesto and add additional salt, black pepper or lemon juice depending on your preference.

Store the pesto in an airtight container in the fridge for up to 10 days.

balsamic mason jar marinade

This marinade is super flavorful and a breeze to toss together. It's so versatile and will soon be your go-to weekend barbecue marinade for your favorite grilled veggies. You can also use this as a lovely vinaigrette. Or you can place about ¼ cup (60 ml) of our Back Porch Mayo (page 134) in a bowl and whisk in 1 tablespoon (15 ml) of this goodness, and you'll have a creamy dressing to drizzle on top of your favorite salad or grilled veggies. So many possibilities in one jar of amazingness! Grab a Mason jar and shake up a batch—happy taste buds await!

yield: 2 cups (480 ml)

1 cup (240 ml) avocado oil
1 cup (240 ml) balsamic vinegar
2 to 4 tbsp (30 to 60 ml) Dijon mustard
1 tsp fine sea salt
½ tsp granulated garlic
½ tsp dried thyme
Black pepper, as needed

In a 20-ounce (600-ml) Mason jar, combine the avocado oil, balsamic vinegar, mustard, salt, garlic, thyme and black pepper. Secure the jar's lid and shake the jar until the ingredients are well blended.

chipotle-tomatillo salsa

This salsa takes two of our favorite ingredients and then does a happy dance on our taste buds. It has layers of smoky yet sweet flavors and is so good that you'll just want to drizzle it on anything that might need a little kick. Chipotle peppers are actually smoked jalapeños, so they can be quite spicy. Pairing them with tomatillos helps tame the heat and lends some great texture. We enjoy this salsa on our Quick 'n' Easy Sausage Breakfast Tacos (page 31), on our Breakfast Enchilada Bake (page 38) or stirred into some creamy smashed avocados for a quick guacamole. Yep, we went there!

yield: 2 cups (480 ml)

5 to 6 cloves garlic, unpeeled and left whole

1 lb (454 g) tomatillos, husked and rinsed

2 to 4 chipotle chilies, rinsed and diced

2 tsp (8 g) coconut sugar

1 tsp fine sea salt

1 tbsp (15 ml) raw honey

1 to 2 tbsp (15 to 30 ml) water, plus additional if needed

In a small cast-iron skillet, dry-roast the garlic, over medium heat, for about 20 minutes, until it has softened and the skins are charred. Remove the skins from the garlic and roughly chop the cloves.

Preheat the broiler. Place the whole tomatillos on a 9½ x 13–inch (24 x 33–cm) baking sheet. Roast the tomatillos under the broiler for approximately 4 minutes, or until they have blistered and their color has dulled. Allow the tomatillos to cool slightly, then remove their stems carefully with a paring knife.

In a large bowl, combine the garlic, tomatillos, chipotle chilies, coconut sugar, salt and honey. Use an immersion blender to completely puree the ingredients. Alternatively, you can use a countertop blender to puree the ingredients.

Check the salsa's consistency. Add the water, 1 tablespoon (15 ml) at a time, to reach your desired consistency.

Store this salsa in an airtight container in the refrigerator for up to 10 days.

creamy sweet onion dip

While this recipe is included in our book to pair with our Crispy Zucchini Fries (page 85) as the ultimate condiment, it is far more than just a dip. The caramelized onions that build the base of this dip possess a unique flavor that is unparalleled. Need to ramp up the flavor of those scrambled eggs? Add a dollop of this dip. Hamburgers on tonight's menu? Use this as your spread instead of mayonnaise. Grilled steak this weekend? You got it—add a dollop. You can even use this as a great topper for baked or roasted potatoes. We bet you'll find so many uses for it, and we couldn't be happier about that.

yield: 1¾ cups (420 ml)

1 medium onion

1 tbsp (12 g) ghee or 1 tbsp (15 ml) avocado oil

¾ cup (180 ml) Back Porch Mayo (page 134)

2 tbsp (30 ml) apple cider vinegar

1 tbsp (15 ml) Dijon mustard

½ tsp fine sea salt

½ tsp black pepper, or as needed

1 tbsp (4 g) finely chopped fresh parsley (optional)

Slice the onion in half and remove the skin and the end with the root. Cut each half into ¾-inch (2-cm)-thick strips.

Heat a 10-inch (25-cm) cast-iron skillet over medium-low heat. Add the ghee and let it melt, then add the onion strips and stir them to coat them with the ghee. Cook the onions for 15 to 20 minutes, stirring them occasionally, until they are golden. Do not increase the heat, as these onions are best cooked low and slow.

Once the onions are done, transfer them to a small plate. Set the plate aside and allow the onions to cool.

In the bowl of a large food processor, combine the Back Porch Mayo, apple cider vinegar, mustard, salt, black pepper and cooled onions. Pulse the food processor until the onions are roughly chopped and the ingredients are combined. If you prefer a completely smooth dip, continue pulsing until the ingredients are completely combined. Add the parsley (if using) and pulse one last time to combine it with the dip.

Transfer the dip to a medium container and store it in the refrigerator for up to 7 days. Use this dip on all the things you might normally use mayonnaise and especially with our Crispy Zucchini Fries (page 85).

mustard vinaigrette

If you're looking for a dressing with some zing, you're in for a treat! This mustard vinaigrette gets some great layers of flavor from the garlic paste you make before whisking all the ingredients together. We feature it as a salad dressing with our Simple and Quick Wedge Salad (page 93) and we use a drizzle for our Dill Pickle Roll-Ups (page 89). This vinaigrette can also be used as a marinade for chicken or shrimp. Make a double batch, so that you have plenty on hand for those afternoons when you find yourself making a fridge-foraging salad for lunch. You'll be glad you did.

yield: approximately 1⅓ cups (319 ml)

½ tsp kosher salt
2 cloves garlic, minced
3 tbsp (45 ml) red wine vinegar
2 tbsp (30 ml) Dijon mustard
1½ tsp (2 g) dried oregano
¼ tsp fine sea salt
Black pepper, as needed (optional)
1 cup (240 ml) avocado oil

To make garlic paste, sprinkle the kosher salt over the garlic. Using a large knife, gather the garlic into a small pile on your cutting board. Holding your knife carefully, press and scrape the blade through the pile of garlic at a slight angle to flatten the garlic. Scrape the garlic back into a pile and repeat this process until it forms a smooth paste.

Place the garlic paste, red wine vinegar, mustard, oregano, salt and black pepper (if using) in a small bowl. Slowly add the avocado oil in a thin stream, whisking the ingredients constantly, until everything is combined well and emulsified. Store this dressing in the refrigerator for up to 10 days.

mango steak sauce

We grill all year long, for several reasons. First, grilling is a great way to transform a regular meal into something special and flavorful. We also grill during the dark days of winter here in Utah, because it reminds our taste buds—and our longing-for-summer souls—that we *can* make it to spring! Steak in all its forms is one of our favorite proteins to grill. This flavorful steak sauce features one of our most favorite fruits—mango. Using a delightfully sweet fruit adds natural sweetness to this steak sauce without all the crazy fillers and sugars in traditional steak sauces.

yield: approximately 1½ cups (360 ml)

½ cup (120 ml) water
¼ cup (40 g) dried organic mangoes
¼ cup (60 ml) plus 2 tbsp (30 ml) balsamic vinegar
⅓ cup (80 ml) organic Worcestershire sauce
¼ cup (60 ml) sugar-free ketchup
¼ cup (60 ml) Dijon mustard
¼ cup (40 g) diced sweet onion
¼ tsp fine sea salt
⅛ tsp black pepper
5 to 6 drops liquid smoke (optional)
Juice of 1 medium lemon

In a small saucepan over medium-high heat, combine the water, mangoes, balsamic vinegar, Worcestershire sauce, ketchup, mustard, onion, salt, black pepper and liquid smoke. Bring the mixture to a boil, reduce the heat to low and let the sauce simmer for 12 to 15 minutes, or until the mangoes are soft.

Remove the saucepan from the heat, and then use an immersion blender or a food processor to puree the ingredients until they form a smooth sauce.

Stir in the lemon juice, then store the sauce in a glass bottle in the refrigerator for up to 2 weeks.

want a drink?

It's almost embarrassing how much of a beverage-loving family we are. For years, we have had a consistent stash of various drinks sitting out in the garage—that's the perfect place to store drinks when you're out of fridge space, if you were wondering. Our stash used to consist of many different sodas, but you've probably already guessed that those have been retired. We could probably write a novel about all the drinks we currently enjoy, but in this chapter we've included just a few of our most favorite recipes that we make on a consistent basis.

One of the highlights of these drinks is that they're all so cute and made with healthy ingredients. It seems silly, but making food look pretty is one of the most enjoyable parts of cooking for us. The Morning Matcha-Mango Latte (page 152) deserves a special shout-out. Going to get a matcha latte from our local coffee shop is one of our favorite pastimes; however, most coffee shops use almond milk, which has stabilizers that upset our stomachs, and matcha that is presweetened with sugar. We decided to make our own and kick it up a notch by adding a delightfully sweet mango puree. This creates an earthy but sweet drink with none of the ingredients that hurt our bodies. Just like coffee shop lattes, this drink is extremely photogenic. Give it a try and have your phone ready to share a picture on social media!

morning matcha-mango latte

Every morning is better with a drink in hand to help you start your day on the right foot. Matcha lattes have been a favorite of ours for quite a few years. They're delightfully cute with their bright green color, and we've grown to love the earthy taste as well as the health benefits matcha has to offer. We thought they couldn't get better until we discovered that matcha pairs incredibly well with one of our other favorite things—mangoes! This mango puree adds such a vibrant flavor and is shockingly photogenic. It adds just the right amount of sweetness, and every morning we're together, we whip up this latte to enjoy.

yield: 2 (10-ounce [300-ml]) servings

1 tsp ceremonial-grade matcha powder

⅔ cup (160 ml) filtered water

1½ cups (248 g) cubed fresh mango

1 tsp raw honey

⅛ tsp fine sea salt

Ice, as needed (optional)

½ cup (120 ml) plain unsweetened almond milk

Sift the matcha powder into a small bowl and add the water. Whisk them together to combine them and create some froth. Set the bowl aside.

Place the mango in a small upright container, then add the honey and salt. Puree the mango with an immersion blender until it is very smooth; you should have 1 cup (240 ml) of puree. Pour ½ cup (120 ml) of the puree into two 16-ounce (480-ml) glasses. Alternatively, you can use a countertop blender or small food processor to create the puree.

Add the ice (if using) and, whisking the matcha again if needed, pour ⅓ cup (80 ml) into each glass. Then, pour ¼ cup (60 ml) of the almond milk into each glass.

Stir the lattes and enjoy!

superfood sipping chocolate

Enjoying a cup of warm chocolate has always been a must for our family. In years past, we will admit, it was a boxed variety loaded with more sugar than actual chocolate and then topped with *more* sugar in the form of tiny marshmallows. We've certainly changed for the better! This recipe is a decadent cup of chocolate that's also loaded with collagen and superfood mushroom powder, so it will provide you with great benefits as well. While you may find it odd to see salt in this recipe, don't skip it. It really brightens up the loveliness of this drink. We decided to call it sipping chocolate, as it's best enjoyed slowly because it's so rich and luxurious. If you prefer a thinner drink, by all means, add a bit more milk and sip away.

yield: 2 (10-ounce [300-ml]) servings

2 cups (480 ml) plain unsweetened almond milk or dairy-free milk of choice

¼ cup (42 g) dairy-free dark chocolate chips

3 tbsp (45 ml) pure maple syrup

1 tsp pure vanilla extract

¼ tsp fine sea salt

2 servings mushroom powder

2 servings collagen peptides

Dairy-free whipped cream (optional)

In a small saucepan over medium-low heat, slowly warm the almond milk. Once the milk is slightly warm, add the chocolate chips, maple syrup, vanilla, salt, mushroom powder and collagen. Whisk these ingredients to combine them.

Continue to warm the chocolate mixture until all of the chocolate chips have melted and the mixture is smooth.

Pour the sipping chocolate into two 10-ounce (300-ml) cups, add a dollop of dairy-free whipped cream (if using), sip and enjoy!

frothy vanilla dream

Yes, this recipe may seem basic on the outside, but the memories it stirs are far from basic. As a young girl growing up in Colorado, Michelle played outside in the snow. Often she'd get hot chocolate when she came inside, but occasionally, she'd request what is lovingly called "Mormon tea"—not an official name, but it certainly has become our family name for it. Momma DeVona would warm up milk, then she'd add vanilla extract and plenty of sugar. Remaking this memory-filled drink was an absolute must for our book. It sings of comfort and is so similar in taste to the original that it's practically indistinguishable. Filled with actual vanilla, it's subtly sweet, and you would never know it's dairy-free.

yield: 2 (10-ounce [300-ml]) servings

3 cups (720 ml) plain unsweetened dairy-free milk of choice

2 servings vanilla collagen peptides

⅛ tsp fine sea salt

⅛ tsp vanilla powder or seeds from 1 vanilla bean

1 tsp pure maple syrup, plus more as needed

In a small saucepan over medium heat, warm the milk, collagen, salt and vanilla powder, stirring the mixture occasionally to incorporate the collagen. Warm the vanilla milk until it is barely simmering—do not allow it to boil. Remove the saucepan from the heat.

Pour the vanilla milk into two 10-ounce (300-ml) mugs. Add the maple syrup, starting with 1 teaspoon and adding more if needed. Grab your trusty frother or a small whisk and, while holding a mug at a slight angle, move the frother up and down for 10 to 15 seconds, until foamy bubbles form. Repeat this process with the other mug of vanilla milk. Sip and enjoy!

birthday peach bellini

It's a long-lived tradition in our family that on someone's birthday, that person gets to pick what's for dinner that night. For many years, there was a particular Italian restaurant that all of Michelle's kids chose to go to for their special days. Of course, a birthday dinner would not be complete without a special drink to go with the meal. The choice always ended up being a virgin peach Bellini—and boy, was it delicious! However, as you could assume, that one was loaded with sugars and syrups that simply aren't friendly to our guts at this point in our lives. We've created this straightforward but no less delicious rendition that we think brings just the right amount of fancy and ease to any special occasion.

yield: 2 (8-ounce [240-ml]) servings

8 oz (224 g) fresh or thawed frozen sliced peaches
1 cup (240 ml) sparkling apple juice
2 (½" [1.3-cm]-thick) slices fresh peaches, for garnishing (optional)
Fresh raspberries, for garnish (optional)

Place the 8 ounces (224 g) of peaches in a medium measuring cup or a narrow widemouthed Mason jar and use an immersion blender to puree them. Alternatively, you can use a blender or small food processor to create this puree. Once the peaches are smooth, divide the puree evenly between two champagne flutes or glasses of your choosing.

Pour ½ cup (120 ml) of the sparkling apple juice into each flute. Use a swizzle stick to mix the peach puree with the apple juice, gently so as not to lose the fizz, until they're combined.

Garnish each glass with 1 slice of peach (if using) and fresh raspberries (if using), and enjoy.

creamy mango-lime smoothie

If a shake and a smoothie had a baby, we think this would be pretty close to what that baby would look like. This creamy smoothie is loosely inspired by the traditional mango lassi that you'll find in almost every Indian-style restaurant. Indian food is something we both love, and ordering a mango lassi to share is definitely one of our favorite "worth it" foods. While that lassi is not Paleo in any way, shape or form, it's a perfect accent to spicy curry, and we've really grown to love the drink as a rare treat. But in order to give our tummies something they'll love more frequently, we developed this dairy-free and refined sugar–free rendition that we absolutely love. It comes together quickly and is delightfully refreshing, especially paired with a spicy meal of your choosing.

yield: 2 (10-ounce [300-ml]) servings

1 cup (165 g) roughly chopped fresh mango

1 cup (240 ml) dairy-free vanilla yogurt

½ cup (120 ml) plain unsweetened almond milk

2 tbsp (30 ml) pure maple syrup

⅛ tsp fine sea salt

Juice of 2 (2-oz [56-g]) limes, plus additional if needed

¼ tsp ground cardamom, plus additional if needed

1 tsp lime zest (optional)

In a deep bowl, combine the mango, yogurt, almond milk, maple syrup, salt, lime juice, cardamom and lime zest (if using). Using an immersion blender, puree the ingredients until everything is smooth and well combined. Alternatively, you can place the ingredients in a blender and puree them.

Taste the smoothie and add more lime juice or cardamom to your liking. Pour the smoothie into two 10-ounce (300-ml) glasses and enjoy.

Resources

We want to provide a bit of brand information and some mini recipes regarding what we use in our kitchen—a sneak peek into our pantry, if you will, so you know what we love and how we develop our recipes. For a full list of brands we love but didn't necessarily use in this book, please have a peek at our cookbook page over on the blog: www.backporchpaleo.com/cookbook.

Brands

Cassava flour: Otto's Naturals. When Otto's hit the grain- and gluten-free world in 2015, we never looked back. We rarely use any other flour in our kitchen these days. All of the recipes in this book that require flour use cassava flour. Tip: When using cassava flour, it is important to fluff it up with a fork before measuring. It is a light flour that settles easily. When measuring, always spoon it into the measuring cup, don't scoop it out of the bag, to ensure accurate amounts.

Coconut sugar: Big Tree Farms. We love using coconut sugar as an unrefined sugar to sub in recipes calling for brown sugar. It lends lovely caramelly undertones to most recipes.

Maple sugar: Coombs Family Farms. We feel that maple sugar is the best sub for granulated sugar in recipes. It's closest in performance, taste and color. We purchase ours in the largest size possible from Amazon, where it is the most affordable we've seen.

Mini Recipes

Porcini mushroom powder: We use this in several of our recipes as an umami flavor boost, and it's easy to make. Simply grind up dried porcini mushrooms in a spice grinder, and you're done! We store ours in a small container in our pantry for up to two years.

Balsamic reduction: A superb accent condiment that you'll find we also use in a couple of recipes in this book. Place 1 cup (240 ml) of balsamic vinegar in a small saucepan over low heat. Simmer the vinegar until it is reduced by half. We store ours in a small lidded container in the pantry for up to six months.

Baking powder: We've been making our own for years as the standard grocery store varieties often contain cornstarch and/or aluminum (#readthelabels). The recipe we use is not our own, so we won't repeat it here, but we will provide the URL to where you can find it: https://thecoconutmama.com/homemade-baking-powder/.

Acknowledgments

This book would not have been possible without the tireless support of our family. They showed up for us in so many ways: as proofreaders, as recipe testers and as moral support. This book was written in the midst of the COVID-19 pandemic, which provided so many challenges we couldn't have anticipated. We are forever grateful for the relationships that we could maintain virtually throughout this process and have cried many grateful tears over the last year. The biggest thanks to our wonderful and loving husbands, Drew and Russell. They have provided constant support in so many ways, allowing us to accomplish this dream together. We love you!

Thank you to our foodie friends who helped us troubleshoot recipes. You know who you are, and we couldn't have created this labor of love without your contributions and moral support. Thank you to our dear friend Ashley Castle— you gave us the strength to put our names to paper when we were at a loss. In photographing this book, the pictures would not be half as beautiful as they are without the incredible pottery from Teri Turner and the entire No Crumbs Left team. Many thanks to all of you.

There are so many shoulders that we have stood on to be where we are today. Danielle Walker and Michelle Tam were the first to inspire this journey. People like Simone Miller and Jennifer Robins are giants in this community and have taught us more about food and being true to ourselves than we ever thought possible.

Of course, thank you to Page Street for allowing us to have this opportunity in the first place. We wouldn't be writing any of these heartfelt messages without our publisher, and for that, we're forever grateful.

Last but not least, we are grateful to our wonderful Back Porch Paleo community on Instagram. We've received so much love and support over the years, and we've grown so many incredible friendships that would otherwise not exist. If not for you, none of this would be possible. This book is just as much for you as it is for us. We can't wait to see what the future holds for all of us.

About the Authors

Michelle Daniels and Makenna Homer are a mother-daughter duo, real-food enthusiasts and the founders of Back Porch Paleo. Shortly after Makenna was diagnosed with Crohn's disease after graduating from high school in 2013, this tiny but mighty duo took her health into their own hands. They chose this Paleo path after months of medical procedures and prescription meds that were just not helping. In the end, Michelle and Makenna were successful, using real food and lots of love with a passion to make sure the healing process was enjoyable and tasty. Their blog was born in early 2015, and nearly 300 recipes later, they are overwhelmed with the sense of community and warm, fuzzy food stories they hear about from followers enjoying their recipes. They could never have imagined that what started as a miserable health crisis could lead to such a wonderful culinary adventure. Michelle and Makenna are foodies, sports fans, lovers of the outdoors and passionate about family as well as making the healing journey enjoyable and delicious.

Index